U.S. THREE-CENT AND FIVE-CENT PIECES

Q. David Bowers

U.S. 3c and 5c Pieces

An Action Guide for the Collector and Investor

by

Q. David Bowers

Bowers and Merena Galleries, Inc.

Other reference books by Q. David Bowers:

Coins and Collectors, United States Half Cents 1793-1857, Early American Car Advertisements, Put Another Nickel In, Guidebook of Automatic Musical Instruments—Vol. I, Guidebook of Automatic Musical Instruments—Vol. II, How to Be a Successful Coin Dealer, Encyclopedia of Automatic Musical Instruments, How to Start a Coin Collection, Collecting Rare Coins for Profit, A Tune for a Token, Adventures With Rare Coins, The History of United States Coinage (for The Johns Hopkins University), *Treasures of Mechanical Music* (with Art Reblitz), *The Postcards of Alphonse Mucha (with Mary Martin), Robert Robinson: American Illustrator, Common Sense Coin Investment, Official ANA Grading Standards for U.S. Coins* (Introduction), *United States Gold Coins: An Illustrated History, Virgil Brand: The Man and His Era, Harrison Fisher* (with Ellen Budd), *United States Copper Coins: An Action Guide for the Collector and Investor,* and *An Inside View of the Coin Hobby in the 1930s: The Walter P. Nichols File.*

BOWERS AND MERENA GALLERIES, INC.
Box 1224
Wolfeboro, NH 03894
(603) 569-5095

ISBN 0-943161-06-1

Catalogues Issued
Sales by Mail Only
(All coins are kept in bank vaults)

Contents

ABOUT THE COVERS: Front: A circa 1905 color postcard shows a carousel at Coney Island, the amusement park wonderland where the nickel was king. Back: Muriel Ostriche, the "Moxie Girl," is shown on a colorful hand-held cardboard fan. At the time, Moxie was available for a nickel a glass at soda fountains.

Credits

The author expresses appreciation to *Coin World* and Margo Russell, editor, for permission to reprint certain information which appeared earlier in the present writer's "Numismatic Depth Study" column in that publication. Albert Bobrofski, Donn Pearlman, Aubrey Bebee, Bernard Nagengast, and Bill Fivaz contributed valuable information. Other credits are given in the text and captions. Typesetting for the book was done by Margaret Graf. Proofreading and graphics work were by Jane E. Scott, Linda Heilig, Sarah Whitten, and Ruth Corrigan. Photography of certain pieces was by Ann Hassin.

About the author: Q. David Bowers, a 1960 graduate of Pennsylvania State University, received in 1976 the Alumni Achievement Award from that institution's College of Business Administration. He served as president of the Professional Numismatists Guild 1977-1979 and is a recipient of the PNG's highest honor, the Founders' Award. A life member (No. 336) of the American Numismatic Association, served as vice-president from 1981 to 1983 and as president from 1983 to 1985. His column, "Numismatic Depth Study," has appeared in *Coin World* for many years and has earned several "Best Columnist" awards given by the Numismatic Literary Guild. Another column appears monthly in *The Numismatist*. His by-line has appeared in all other major numismatic publications, including *Numismatic News*, *Coins Magazine*, and *CoinAge*. He has written the numismatic section of the *Encyclopedia Americana* and has written two dozen books. With Raymond N. Merena, the author owns one of America's leading rare coin businesses, Bowers and Merena Galleries, Inc.

LIBERTY
13
F

Introduction

This book, one in a series covering American coinage, discusses three-cent and five-cent pieces. To be more precise, the subjects are nickel three-cent pieces, silver three-cent pieces, nickel five-cent pieces (commonly called simply "nickels"), and silver half dimes.

During the Civil War, when the outcome of the conflict between the North and South was uncertain, specie or hard money of all kinds was hoarded. Filling the gap were many privately-issued substitutes, including the innovative encased postage stamps of John Gault, paper fractional currency notes issued by the government, scrip notes issued by merchants and other private interests, and thousands of different varieties of cent-size tokens. In 1865 and 1866 the government desired to produce coins that would not be hoarded but yet would be of higher value than the bronze cent and two-cent pieces. Thus born of necessity was the nickel three-cent denomination of 1865 and the nickel five-cent piece a year later. Made of copper and nickel alloy, the coins were intended to have low intrinsic value. It was believed, probably rightly so, that such denominations, if made of silver, would simply be hoarded or melted.

Although the nickel three-cent piece faded from view less than 25 years later, the nickel-five cent piece became a staple of American coinage. The Shield design, followed in succession by the Liberty, Buffalo, and Jefferson types saw wide circulation in the channels of commerce. Then, as the hobby of coin collecting developed, examples became highly cherished by numismatists.

While such landmark scarcities and rarities as the 1877 and 1878 Shield nickels, the awesome 1913 Liberty nickel, and others have occupied pages of print, to my way of thinking there is something appealing about a *well worn* five-cent piece. Such a coin has seen action, it has been on the front line, it did its duty and shows it. Indeed, countless peep-show machines, trolley cars, merry-go-rounds, coin-operated pianos, and other mechanical marvels of yesteryear would have ground to a silent halt were it not for the ubiquitous nickel. A pocketful of Liberty nickels in 1900, or 1910, or 1916 opened the door

Facing page: Q. David Bowers.

to all sorts of magical treasures, just as a pocketful of large copper cents a century earlier furnished the passport to many enjoyments in life.

The silver three-cent denomination, minted from 1851 through 1873, comprises three distinct design types and enough rarities to satisfy every numismatist. From a technical viewpoint, the first silver three-cent pieces, those of the 1851-1853 years, are unique in American coinage in that they are composed of .750 parts silver and .250 parts copper, instead of the regulation .900 silver and .100 copper—a nice technical point for a quiz at your next coin club meeting! Interestingly, silver three-cent pieces were forgotten by many numismatists until around 1960, when collecting by design types became especially popular. Since that time, the series has been on the "most wanted list" of many collectors.

The half dime is one of America's most interesting coins. Extending from 1794 until 1873, the series experienced growth of American coinage technology from the early days of hand-cut dies to the later period of high-speed presses. Along the way many interesting overdates, errors, recuttings, and other varieties were produced.

How much is it worth? How rare is it? These two questions are apt to be the first asked by many collectors. Additional questions such as: How many were minted? Who designed it? Why is it appealing to collectors? What is its history?— are asked less frequently. To answer the question of value, there are many publications to choose from. Some, like the *Guide Book of United States Coins,* endeavor to *report* values. Others, such as a myriad of popular newsletters, attempt to *predict* prices—with varying degrees of success. Often left waiting far behind are answers to questions concerning design, numismatic appeal, technology, and so on. While one can argue that coin prices are interesting, I suggest that art, history, romance, and other considerations comprise the main body of what is interesting to the numismatist. And, I posit that the study of these factors will put you in a better position to understand the most popular of all categories: worth (or price, or value, or whatever you want to call it). Although many modern market gurus are hesitant to admit it, the greatest financial profits in the coin collecting game have always gone to those with the most knowledge—and knowledge means more than simply what Coin "X" sold for last Tuesday afternoon.

For the investor or collector, or the person who both collects and invests (an ideal combination!), the present book will undoubtedly lead to *action* that might not take place if you did not read the text. You will learn that certain coins are true *sleepers* and are not recognized for the rarities they are. A coin can be common in one grade and a great rarity in another, the vagaries of striking play a part, design elements are important—these and many other aspects are discussed.

Production of coins at the Philadelphia Mint Circa 1904

The book now in your hands is envisioned as a part of a "bookshelf" or "library" of monographs on the subject of American coinage—ranging from early colonial issues through the entire federal series from half cents through double eagles, then to commemoratives, patterns, tokens and medals, and paper money. Each volume, in my opinion, will make an ideal companion to your favorite price guide, newsletter, or other source of market value information. At the same time, each volume can help you appreciate coins more than ever and lead to an understanding which may well bring you monetary profit.

In my mind's eye I think of the present book as a "fireside chat" (as I put it in an earlier volume, *United States Copper Coins*) a conversation with the author. "Dave, tell me all about Liberty nickels—which issues are rare, how were they used, what do you know about them? Pretend that you and I are in a cozy lodge—perhaps up in the Rocky Mountains, perhaps deep in the woods of New England, perhaps amidst southern pines—and we have an evening to "talk coins." Let's do it through the pages in the present book!

—Q. David Bowers
January 1985

IN GOD WE TRUST
1866
STATES OF AMERICA
5
CENTS

Collecting Nickel Three-Cent Pieces

1865-1889

COLLECTING NICKEL THREE-CENT PIECES 1865-1889

The series of nickel three-cent pieces is an interesting one for the collector. It is rather brief in duration, contains no "impossible" rarities (although several are elusive), and pieces can be collected in high grades without much difficulty, assuming that one has a satisfactory balance in a checking account. As is the case with certain other issues, most nickel three-cent pieces go to those forming type sets, numismatists who seek but a single example. However, over the years numerous specialists have formed date runs.

Why were nickel three-cent pieces made? There were several reasons. In 1865, when they were first issued, the Civil War had ended, but silver coins were still hoarded by the public. Newly minted silver coins were not released by the government but were kept in Treasury vaults, for to have released them would have just provided profits for speculators. The nickel three-cent piece was intended to provide a medium of exchange. Made of nickel alloy, it had little intrinsic or melt-down value and thus was not a candidate for hoarding. Another reason for the issue was to provide a convenient method to buy three-cent postage stamps. Most small transactions at the time, and for a number of years thereafter, were effected by fractional currency notes, issued in denominations of 3c, 5c, 10c, 15c, 25c, and 50c. The public derisively referred to these as "stamps."

First minted in 1865, three-cent pieces of nickel alloy were issued through 1889. Following the trend of other ephemeral nineteenth-century denominations, mintage figures reveal that great hopes were held for the new coins. During the first year more than 11 million pieces were struck. Such a high figure was never to be obtained again. The following year saw a mintage of just below 5 million pieces. With a few bumps in the coinage graph, mintages trended downward through the end of the series. By 1877 the demand was so slight that coinage consisted only of Proof examples struck for collectors. From that year through 1889 business strike mintages of nickel three-cent pieces were negligible except for one year, 1881, in which approximately one million were produced.

The design of the nickel three-cent piece features the head of Miss Liberty facing to the left. A similar style was envisioned for use on the one-cent piece and also on the nickel five-cent piece. Patterns were prepared for these other two denominations. However, except for the three-cent piece, no others were ever made for circulation.

The reverse of the nickel three-cent piece displays the Roman numeral III enclosed by a laurel wreath. The wreath was copied, more or less, from the 1859 Indian cent.

From the outset of its production, the hard nickel composition of the three-cent piece presented striking problems. As a result, many nickel three-cent pieces, particularly those of the earlier years (1865-1876) are weakly struck. This is usually most evident in the fine vertical bands that are part of the Roman numeral design on the reverse. Even a piece sharply struck in other areas is apt to have weakness in this feature.

The weakness was caused by several situations. First, the nickel alloy was hard, and great difficulties were encountered in having the coin strike up sharply. Second, the Roman numeral appeared on the reverse opposite the corresponding part of the obverse on which the Liberty head appeared. The metal from the planchet had to flow in two directions to fill both features. Third, to minimize die wear and to facilitate striking, the dies were not spaced as closely as they could have been, thus lessening the metal flow.

The same situation occurs quite frequently elsewhere throughout coinage history. The requirement of metal flow in two directions was a problem with flying eagle cents. The 1921 Peace dollar is even a better known example; the relief was simply too high on the obverse to fill in the details of the hair strands properly while, at the same time, filling in the eagle on the reverse. Nor is the problem confined to the United States. Certain twentieth-century English pennies of King George V show evidence of the same situation: the metal could not properly fill the king's portrait on one side and the Britannia figure on the other side. The design was subsequently modified.

Had the Mint modified the nickel three-cent design so that Miss Liberty would have been in very shallow relief, then probably most nickel three-cent pieces seen today would be sharply struck. The Peace dollar design was modified after the 1921 coinage proved unsatisfactory, and in an even more famous instance the High Relief MCMVII double eagles of 1907 were modified to a shallower format.

Dies wore quickly during coinage of the nickel three-cent denomination. Once a die lost detail, the Mint often strengthened certain parts,

NICKEL THREE-CENT PIECES

Nickel three-cent pieces were produced from 1865 through 1889. All of the issues are of one design, as shown above. The series contains but a single unusual variety, the 1887/6 overdate, which is distinctive as occurring in Proof preservation (very few Proof overdates were made in American coinage history). Curiously, at least two overdate dies were made, one of which was used to produce business strikes.

The nickel three-cent piece was issued with great expectations, but it subsequently developed that the first year of issue, 1865, was also the year of greatest production. The mintage quantity of 11,382,000 that year was not even closely approached by any other year. By the late 1870s, the denomination was unwanted by the banks and the public. With the exception of 1881, mintages were low from that point forward. Today, the 1877 (made only in Proof condition, presumably to the extent of just 510 pieces), the 1878, and the 1886, all Proof-only dates, are considered to be rare. Numerous other dates of the same era are likewise very elusive.

Today, the main demand for nickel three-cent pieces comes from those forming type sets who desire but a single specimen of the 1865-1889 design. However, as there are no "impossible" rarities, numerous collectors have found it a challenge to assemble one of each date, plus the overdate, plus in some instances both numeral varieties of 1873 (closed 3 and open 3).

Close-up of 1887/6 overdate

particularly the date, by repunching. This caused a great proliferation of recut or re-engraved dates and other features. The same situation occurred to an even greater extent with early pieces in the shield nickel series.

A number of issues are scarce among nickel three-cent pieces. Examples from the first year of striking, 1865, are very common in worn grades, are seen regularly in Uncirculated grade, but are elusive in Proof. This double standard of rarity is caused by the fact that nickel three-cent pieces were not produced until later in the year by which time many 1865 Proof sets had been distributed without pieces of this style. The same situation is responsible for the rarity of a number of other series during the first year of issue, including the Proof 1866 shield nickel.

Pieces of 1877, 1878, and 1886 were struck only in Proof condition. No business strikes were made. 1878 nickel three-cent pieces often occur with a full frosty "Uncirculated" or business strike appearance, but as these were originally struck as Proofs and were included as part of the Proof sets of that year, they are designated as Proofs by cataloguers today. Were it not for the Proof status as evidenced by Mint reports, these Uncirculated-appearing pieces would not be described as Proof.

This raises an interesting question: Is a coin a Proof because it was designated by the Mint as such, or is a coin a Proof only in a *prima facie* sense? In other words, if a coin appears to be a Proof, then is it a Proof? If a coin is supposed to be a Proof, but it doesn't look like one, then is it Uncirculated rather than Proof? This is a point left open for personal debate, for there is no uniformity of opinion among numismatists.

In a somewhat related situation the Royal Canadian Mint for many years produced special "specimen" sets for collectors. These pieces contained coins with mirrorlike surfaces struck from highly polished dies. However, Canadian Mint officials insisted repeatedly that no Proofs were being made by that institution. That the pieces were special was acknowledged, but that they were Proofs was denied. And yet each piece bore every earmark of a Proof!

One of the most curious of all nickel three-cent pieces is the 1887/6 overdate. This piece is remarkable as being one of the few United States overdates to exist in Proof format. It was considered to be the only readily collectible Proof overdate until around 1970 when the first 1879/8 shield nickel was publicized. Interestingly, at least two different dies were made of the 1887/6 nickel three-cent piece. One variety was struck in Proof, but another variety, microscopically different in the placement of the last two digits in relation to each other, is known only in business strike form. The latter variety has received very little publicity over the years.

Obverse and reverse views of an 1885 nickel three-cent piece.

Nickel three-cent pieces of the 1877-1889 years have long been favorites with collectors and investors alike. Although enough Proofs were made to satisfy most requirements, a certain fascination can be had by contemplating low mintage figures. For example, the mintage of just 4,790 pieces for the year 1885 (divided into 3,790 Proofs plus 1,000 business strikes) is infinitely more appealing than the mintage quantity for 1865: 11,382,000! Low mintage does not a rarity make, but some connection will undoubtedly always exist between low mintage and high market price.

For the collector contemplating collecting nickel three-cent pieces by dates, several possibilities exist:

Obtaining one of each date from 1865 through 1889, plus the 1887/6 overdate, for the least expense, will result in a mixture of low and high grade pieces. Issues from 1865 through 1876 are readily available in well-worn grades and cost little. Although Good and Very Good grades are the least expensive of all, total expense is not great. A goal of Fine, Very Fine or Extremely Fine examples is more advisable. Beginning with the year 1877, specimens, except for the year 1881 (and to a lesser extent the years 1888 and 1889), are usually seen only in higher grades. Because 1877, 1878, and 1886 pieces were struck only in Proof condition, the buyer must choose between either a minimal-condition Proof (Proof-60) or a Proof that has seen circulation. In practice, few circulated Proofs exist of these dates, so Proof-60 is a reasonable objective. Lower grade examples of 1879, 1880, 1882, 1883, 1884, 1885, and 1887, while they turn up from time to time, are nearly as rare as the proverbial hen's teeth or a guinea pig's tail—not quite, but almost. Probably the best objective for collecting specimens from these years would be to acquire Proof-60 examples or impaired Proofs, considering yourself lucky if a few scattered pieces can be obtained in grades from Fine through AU. Although pricing guides list such grades as Good and Very Good, such dates were made toward the end of the series, and most did not survive in circulation long enough to be worn that extensively.

The dates 1881, 1888, and 1889 are obtainable in worn grades, so Fine to Extremely Fine examples represent a good collecting objective. 1881, with a mintage of 1,080,575, is actually one of the commoner dates in the series.

For the numismatist who aspires to assemble a collection of Uncirculated and Proof examples, then a reasonable goal would be to obtain one each of the dates from 1865 through 1876 in Uncirculated grade (taking care to obtain sharp strikes wherever one is available), one each of the years 1877 through 1880 in Proof preservation, an 1881 Uncirculated, and 1882 through 1889 in Proof. Certain issues in the 1880s appear in Uncirculated condition from time to time, but with the ex-

1866 VG $1.00; Fine $2.25; VF $3.00; EF 4.00
1867 Good $.85; VG $1.25; Brilliant Unc. 12.50
1868 VG $1.00; Fine $2.00; VF 3.25
1869 VG $1.40; VF $3.00; EF 4.75
1870 Very Good 1.50
1871 VG-Fine 3.25
1872 Very Fine 26.00
1873 Very rare. Brilliant Proof 165.00

NICKEL THREE-CENT PIECES

1865 AU, sharply double-cut date 4.00
1866 AU $2.50; Brilliant Proof 42.50
1867 Brilliant Proof 20.00
1868 VF $1.25; Brilliant Proof 24.00
1869 Fine $1.25; Brilliant Proof 22.50
1870 VF $1.50; Brilliant Unc. 5.75
1871 Good 1.00
1872 VF $2.25; Brilliant Uncirculated $9.00; Brilliant Proof 23.50
1873 Fine 1.25; AU 3.00; Brilliant Proof 17.00
1874 Fine $2.00; EF $3.50; Brilliant Uncirculated 10.50; Brilliant Proof 22.00
1875 Good $2.00; EF $6.00; Brilliant Uncirculated 16.00
1876 VG $2.00; Brilliant Proof 25.50
1877 Brilliant Proof. Rare 195.00
1878 Brilliant Proof. Scarce. Special Price 60.00
1879 Brilliant Proof 14.50
1880 Brilliant Proof 14.00
1881 Fine or better $.75; Brilliant Unc. $4.25; Brilliant Proof 11.00
1882 Fine 3.50; Brilliant Proof 14.00
1883 Brilliant Proof 13.50
1884 Brilliant Proof 14.00
1885 Brilliant Proof 14.50
1886 Brilliant Proof 14.50
1887/6 Overdate. Brilliant Proof 69.50
1888 EF 4.75; Brilliant Proof 13.00
1889 Brilliant Proof 13.50

SILVER THREE-CENT PIECES

1851 VG $1.50; Fine $2.75; Brilliant Uncirculated 15.00
1851-O Good 4.00; EF $13.50; Brilliant Uncirculated 37.50
1852 EF $3.50; Brilliant Uncirculated 9.00
1853 VF $2.75; Brilliant Uncirculated 9.00
1854 Fine 4.50
1855 rare date. VG 7.50; Fine $15.00 VF 16.50
1859 Fine 4.25
1860 AU, brilliant 7.50
1862 AU $6.00; Brilliant Unc. $8.50; Brilliant Proof 21.50
1873 Brilliant Proof. Here's an undervalued item. Although it is equally as rare as the two-cent piece of the same date the 1873 silver three-cent piece sells for less than half the price. 59.50

NICKELS

1866 first year. with rays. Abt. G $.90; Good $1.25; Very Fine $7.00; Extremely Fine 9.00
1867 with rays. One of the scarcest coins in this set. Abt. G. $3.50; Very Fine 19.00
1867 no rays. Extremely Fine $3.00; Brilliant Proof, scarce 34.00
1868 Very Fine 2.50
1870 Fair $.75; Good 1.75
1871 Abt. G. clear date $12.50; **Brilliant Uncirculated,** a gem. Rare 105.00
1871 Brilliant Proof 147.50
1874 Fair 1.50; Brilliant Proof 44.00
1875 Brilliant Proof. rare 83.50
1876 Fair $1.50; Good $3.25; EF $9.00; Brilliant Proof 27.00
1878 Brilliant Proof. Should be an excellent investment as this date and the 1877 are the only nickels from 1866 to date that were coined in Proof only—none for circulation 82.50
1879 Brilliant Proof. fairly scarce 29.00
1880 Fine, seldom seen in circulated condition $12.00; Brilliant Proof 35.00
1881 Fine $9.00; Brilliant Proof 29.00
1882 VG $1.25; Fine $2.50; Brilliant Proof 14.00
1883 shield. VF $2.75; EF $3.75; Brilliant Proof 13.50

Liberty type

1883 with CENTS. Good $2.00; Brilliant Unc. 13.50
1884 Good 2.25
1885 G-VG 37.50
1886 Good $13.50; Brilliant Uncirculated, rare 47.50
1887 VG $1.50; Fine 3.00
1888 Fine $5.50; Brilliant Proof 19.00
1890 Fine 3.50

A 1959 page from "Empire Topics," a priced catalogue issued by the author. The rarest date in the nickel three-cent series, the 1877, commanded a price of $195 in Proof state, while a Proof 1873 silver three-cent piece fetched $59.50, and a Proof 1878 Shield nickel was offered at $82.50.

ception of 1881 and, to a much lesser degree, 1888 and 1889, all are rarities. In fact, upon close inspection most "Uncirculated" issues of such dates as 1880, 1882, 1883, 1884, and 1885 are simply Proofs with a degree of mint lustre. The Mint was not fastidious about producing completely mirrorlike surfaces during this era, and numerous Proofs are somewhat frosty. This is why 1878 nickel three-cent pieces in particular, coins struck only as Proofs, often appear to be "Uncirculated."

Still another way to form a complete date set is to acquire a complete set of Proofs from 1865 through 1889. The major rarity in the series is 1865. This apparently is the lowest-mintage date because these pieces were first produced well into the year 1865, by which time many Proof sets had been distributed without this denomination. 1877, 1878, and 1887/6 are expensive due to their popularity and rarity. Many of the other issues, although they differ considerably in rarity from each other, are priced about the same—the main demand for them is for inclusion in type sets. Proof issues with correspondingly low business strike mintages (1879, 1880, 1882, 1883, 1884, 1885, 1886, and 1887) are apt to be priced slightly higher due to the increased interest in the pieces. Low mintage figures are forever fascinating to the numismatist!

Attractive Choice Proof issues are scarce, particularly for years prior to 1877. Although these earlier years are, for the most part, not expensive (1865 being an exception), fewer Choice Proofs remain than do of the later dates. At one time Abe Kosoff tried to corner the market on Proof 1866 nickel-three cent pieces. After spending several years buying examples of this date he had gathered only several dozen pieces. He noted that the coins were at least three or four times harder to find than were Proofs of most dates in the 1880s.

If a single nickel three-cent piece is sought for a type set, the choices are many. Proofs candidates include just about any date except 1865, 1877, 1878, or 1887/6, which tend to be more expensive. There is a "fun" aspect about owning an issue in the 1880s, for the related business strike mintage figure is very low. Such coins are easily available, for thousands of Proofs were made of nearly every date. As time goes on, Choice Proofs will become increasingly elusive, for surviving specimens continue to fall prey to cleaning and other "improvements." Also, the surface of nickel three-cent pieces is chemically active and tends to develop flecks or spots over a period of time, especially if the coins are stored in damp conditions.

Nickel three-cent pieces: an interesting series. Good luck with your search!

Open Letter From Mr. Bullowa

NATIONAL COIN WEEK

MARCH 30, TO APRIL 6, 1940

SPONSORED BY THE

AMERICAN NUMISMATIC ASSOCIATION

DAVID M. BULLOWA, Chairman

95 FIFTH AVENUE

NEW YORK, N. Y.

January 8, 1940.

Dear Friend and Collector:

This letter is addressed to you, because we would like to have your cooperation in the observance of NATIONAL COIN WEEK.

Our purpose is to stimulate collecting by creating new collectors, and through the use of displays and announcements present to the public our hobby.

We also wish to further the scope of the American Numismatic Association, and bring new readers to the pages of its official magazine the "Numismatist".

We believe this can be best accomplished by the following activities during COIN WEEK.

1. Numismatic exhibits by individuals and clubs in your community during COIN WEEK. Several well-located displays all properly labelled. Exhibit a current copy of the "Numismatist".
2. Accurate newspaper publicity about interesting numismatic items, connected if possible, with your locality.
3. Arrange a radio program at your local station.
4. Announce if possible, where and when, free information about coins may be obtained in your community, as well as information about the American Numismatic Association.

The suggested themes about which 1940 COIN WEEK programs throughout the country might be centered are:

1. THREE CENT NICKEL PIECES: (1865-1940)
   The first coinage of this series took place in 1865. It is fitting to observe in 1940 the Diamond Jubilee of this numismatic event.
   Why not include in every COIN WEEK exhibit a few coins of this denomination, with appropriate comments about the use of this nickel series.
2. COIN OR TREASURY NOTES: (1890-1940)
   In 1890 the first issue of United States Coin or Treasury notes was authorized. In 1940 we mark the Golden anniversary of this issue. There is no doubt that it is one of the most interesting issues of our paper money.
   If possible examples should be included in the displays.

CONTRIBUTE YOUR SHARE TO THE SUCCESS OF 1940 COIN WEEK.

Nickel three-cent pieces were one of two themes suggested for Coin Week in 1940 as noted in this announcement from David M. Bullowa, chairman of the event.

STANDARD CATALOGUE
OF
UNITED STATES
COINS AND CURRENCY

1938 EDITION

READY SEPTEMBER 27th

The popular interest in coin collecting and frequent price changes make it imperative for all collectors of United States coins to have this book. It lists and describes all United States coins and currency and gives the prices at which most of them may be purchased from the publishers. Includes: Early American Coins, 1652-1796; United States Gold, Silver and Copper Coins; Private Gold Issues, 1830-1861; Commemorative Coins; Early Colonial and Continental Notes; United States Notes; Fractional Currency; Confederate and Southern States Notes. Contains over 900 illustrations.

Large octavo, cloth, bound uniform with the Standard Postage Stamp Catalogue.

Price $2.50

Postage extra. Shipping weight 2 lbs.

Distributed by

SCOTT STAMP & COIN CO.

1 West 47th Street — **New York**

Until the advent of the "Guide Book of United States Coins" in 1946, the "Standard Catalogue," published by Wayte Raymond, reigned supreme as the standard pricing guide. In the days before collecting by design types achieved wide popularity, most numismatist aspired to own date runs of nickel three-cent pieces, nickel five-cent pieces, half dimes, and other series.

PRICE CHANGES IN THE STANDARD PRICE LIST OR CATALOGUE

SMALL CENTS

Date	Fine	Unc.	Proof
1859			4.00
1860			4.00
1861	.75		
1862			3.00
1863			3.50
1864 C. N.	.35	1.00	
1864 Br.	.35	2.50	7.50
1870	1.50		
1871	2.00		
1873			3.00
1874			3.50
1875			3.50
1880			1.25
1881			1.25
1882			1.25
1883			1.25
1884			1.25
1885			2.00
1887			1.25
1888			1.25
1889			1.25
1890			1.25
1891			1.25
1892			1.25
1893		1.00	1.50
1894			1.50
1895			1.50
1896			1.50
1897		1.00	1.50
1899		1.00	1.50
1900		1.00	1.50
1901		1.00	1.50
1908 S		3.00	
1909 S		6.00	

LINCOLN

Date	Unc.
1912 S	2.00
1915 D	1.25
1925 S	4.00

TWO CENT PIECES

Date	Proof
1872	6.00
1873	20.00

THREE CENT PIECES

Date	Unc.	Proof
1877		15.00
1881	.75	1.50
1882	1.00	1.50
1883	1.00	1.50
1884	1.00	1.50
1885	1.00	1.50
1886	1.00	1.50
1887	2.00	3.00
1888	.75	1.25
1889	1.00	1.25

FIVE CENT PIECES

Date	Unc.	Proof
1867	1.25	
1868	1.25	
1869	1.50	
1871	3.50	5.00
1872	2.00	3.00
1876	1.50	2.50
1878		10.00
1883 Cents	1.00	2.00
1884	1.00	1.25
1885	1.50	2.00
1886	1.50	2.00
1887	1.00	1.25
1888	1.25	1.50
1889	1.25	1.50
1890	1.00	1.25
1891		1.25
1892		1.25
1893		1.50
1894		1.25
1895	1.00	1.25
1896	1.00	1.25
1897	1.00	1.50
1898	1.00	1.50
1899	1.00	1.50
1900	1.00	1.50
1901	1.00	1.50
1902	1.00	1.50
1903	1.00	1.50
1904	1.00	1.50
1905	1.00	1.50
1906	1.00	1.50
1913 S Type II	7.50	
1926 S	7.50	
1927 S	15.00	

TWENTY CENT PIECES

Date	Proof
1877	17.50
1878	17.50

In 1939 Wayte Raymond, publisher of "The Standard Catalogue of United States Coins," issued a list of price changes. The figures, even for scarcer dates, are laughably low compared to what the same pieces would sell for several decades later.

Collecting Silver Three-Cent Pieces

1851-1873

COLLECTING SILVER THREE-CENT PIECES
1851-1873

Type of 1851-1853

Silver three-cent pieces were authorized by Congress on March 3, 1851. Ease of purchasing three-cent postage stamps was given as a reason for producing this new denomination. Most collectors today refer to these small coins simply as "silver three-cent pieces," although from time to time the term *trime* has been used, including in Mint correspondence.

Silver three-cent pieces coined from 1851 through 1853 inclusive bear a six-pointed star on the obverse and the Roman numeral III enclosed by an ornamental C-shaped device on the reverse. Prior to the issuance of pieces for circulation in 1851, patterns of varying designs were produced at the Mint. One of these patterns, described at the time as the ugliest of all American coins, is very simple in design: the obverse bears nothing but a 3 and the reverse consists only of III.

Whereas the standard for United States silver coins was an alloy consisting of nine parts silver and one part copper (the copper adding strength), silver three-cent pieces of the 1851-1853 years were made of a new composition consisting of 7½ parts silver and 2½ parts copper. 1854 and later issues reverted to the normal standard used for other silver denominations.

The most interesting early piece is the 1851-O issue produced at the New Orleans Mint. This particular coin has the distinction of being the only silver three-cent piece produced at a mint other than Philadelphia. In fact, it has an even greater distinction: it is the only piece of a denomination of less than five cents to be produced with a mintmark during the nineteenth century! In deference to readers who are interested in numismatic trivia, in 1837 some large cents were struck at the New Orleans Mint to test the dies. Unfortunately for collectors today, these did not bear mintmarks, so 1837-O cents are not a reality. It is not known if any examples were saved once die testing was completed.

From 1851 through 1853 more than 30 million silver three-cent pieces were produced, more than were made during all of the remaining years of the series from 1854 until the end in 1873! The slumping in interest in this denomination is similar to the trend in the two-cent and nickel three-cent series.

Examples of 1851-1853 coins are available in all grades from Good through Uncirculated. In the latter grade 1851-O is considerably scarcer than the others, due primarily to its substantially lower mintage. Sharp striking was not a feature of this issue, and often the details are not well defined, particularly at the center of the obverse and the corresponding part of the reverse, due to metal flow requirements.

Type of 1854-1858

In 1854 the design was modified to include three outlines around the obverse star. The metallic composition was changed to nine parts silver and one part copper. Coins of this style were made from 1854 through 1858 inclusive.

Of all three types of the silver three-cent denomination, the 1854-1858 style is the most difficult to locate. Few Uncirculated pieces were saved at the time of issue, so pieces in Mint State are quite rare today. At the tail end of the series, 1858, Proofs were just beginning to be distributed to collectors. In that year 80 Proof sets were made, each with a coin of this denomination. Proofs were made from 1854 through 1857 as well, but fewer than two dozen are known of each of these dates. Thus, a type set or date set collector desiring a top grade piece cannot readily obtain Proofs, nor are Uncirculated coins easy to find.

Business strike examples of the 1854-1858 design are usually found weakly struck, often with parts of the lettering flat around the borders and with indistinct centers. This is quite normal for the style. Of the five dates in this range, 1854 and 1855 are *occasionally* seen as better strikes, but even these usually are not extremely sharp. 1856, 1857, and 1858 are nearly always extremely weak. A numismatist seeking sharply struck pieces is apt to have a lot of empty spaces in his collection! This brings up another point: When seeking coins for your collection it is important to have reasonable expectations and to know what the possibilities of obtaining coins in certain grades and certain degrees of striking. Perhaps after reading this book you will know, for example, that an auction listing such as "1857 silver three-cent piece, sharply struck, extremely rare" would indeed represent a piece of great rarity, whereas a listing of "1861 silver three-cent piece, sharply struck, extremely rare" would indicate that the cataloguer was not very familiar with the series! Many of the things related to you through the pages of this book I have learned by experience, sometimes costly. Just as Dr. Sheldon wrote his *Penny Whimsy* book because he always wanted to read it and it wasn't there, one of my reasons for writing this book

1855 (enlarged two diameters)

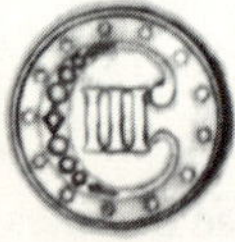

This representative group of Type I silver three-cent pieces includes 1851, 1851-O, and 1853. The 1851-O, minted at New Orleans, is the only branch mint issue of the denomination. The pieces of the 1851-1853 design were considered to be too small for convenient handling, so the size was subsequently increased (see following).

Silver three-cent pieces of the 1854-1858 increased-diameter format. On the Type II design the star was given outlines, and other minor changes were made. Difficulties were experienced in striking the pieces up properly, with the result that nearly all examples seen today are exceedingly weak, particularly around the border. Pieces illustrated here are exceptions and are selected from among dozens of others.

Representative examples of the Type III silver three-cent piece design used 1859-1873. The pieces shown here are Proofs.

Shown on this page are examples of the three major design types of silver three-cent pieces: Type I (1851-1853), Type II (1854-1858), and Type III (1859-1873). Among the early pieces, 1851-O is the scarcest and has a mintage which is but a tiny fraction of the others. All Type II silver three-cent pieces are scarce, and the 1855, with the lowest mintage in the series, is especially so. However, the author found that in Choice Uncirculated grade the rarities were different, and 1856 emerged as the most elusive of the type. Although the mintage of 139,000 1855 silver three-cent pieces as compared to 1,458,000 dated 1856 illustrates the relative rarity of worn pieces, in Uncirculated grade the writer has handled more pieces dated 1855! Why are 1856 silver three-cent pieces rare in Uncirculated grade? Here is a numismatic mystery.

There are numerous scarce issues among Type III issues, including all dates of the 1863-1873 span. However, Proofs were struck of those years, and the demand for dates is usually filled by a Proof example, specimens of which were specifically set aside by collectors at the time of issue.

is to let others read what I would have given an eyetooth to have read years ago!

In worn grades, the availability of silver three-cent pieces of the different dates from 1854 through 1858 is approximately proportional to the mintage figures. Thus, 1855 pieces, with a mintage of 139,000, are about ten times rarer than those of 1856, which have a posted figure of 1,458,000. Of course, most silver three-cent pieces of all years have long since disappeared, but those that do survive exist in proportion to the numbers originally made. Curiously, in Uncirculated grade the situation is different. It is my experience that the great rarity among 1854 to 1858 silver three-cent pieces in Mint State is the 1856. This observation did not come about until pictures were being selected for this book. In reviewing the historical files of Bowers and Merena Galleries, Inc., and the predecessor firm Bowers and Ruddy Galleries, Inc., I was able to find numerous auction catalogue and price list photographs of Uncirculated 1854, 1855, 1857, and 1858 coins, but just a solitary 1856! To be candid, I had completely overlooked the rarity of the 1856, believing it to be relatively plentiful—based upon the generous original mintage. However, obviously this is far from the truth. Here is a sleeper. In terms of rarity a Choice Uncirculated 1856 apparently is *several times* rarer than the 1855 (the date which is normally considered to be the most elusive).

Type of 1859-1873

In 1859 the design was revised again. The Mint realized that pieces were not striking up properly, so the star outlines were changed from three to two, and other minor changes were made. While this did not completely end the problem, for dies spaced ever so slightly further apart than they should have been on certain issues still caused lightness of impression, most silver three-cent pieces of 1859 and later years are nevertheless quite sharp. Indeed, weakly struck pieces are the exception.

Mintages were fairly liberal from 1859 through 1862, when the futility of striking coins became apparent, for specie (hard money or coins) payments had been suspended, and any pieces struck would simply go into Treasury vaults. So, from that point forward relatively few were made. Most often seen today in Uncirculated grade are pieces dated 1860, and, in particular, 1861 and 1862. Although 1859 has a substantially larger mintage than either 1860 or 1862, in Uncirculated grade it is much rarer. This is just one of those "nice things to know"—information which experienced numismatists use now and then to acquire rarities for no more than one has to pay for a commoner issue.

Worn specimens of silver three-cent pieces of all years from 1851 through 1862 (embracing all three design types) exist in relative proportion to the original mintage quantities. The lower mintage issues are the scarcer examples, as might be expected. On the other hand, the survival of Uncirculated pieces was strictly a matter of chance. Throughout American coinage some issues were saved in greater numbers than were others. Original mintages, while playing a part, do not conclusively determine rarity.

Among earlier issues of the Type 3 silver three-cent pieces are two overdates. The first is 1862/1, minted in business strike form and quite often seen (although scarcer than an 1862 issue without this feature). The second is the 1863/2 Proof. This, too, is scarcer than its regular date counterpart.

From 1863 through 1873 relatively few business strikes were produced. Each year Proofs were made for inclusion in sets, and it is these

Proofs that are most often seen today. For example, Mint reports indicate that 1,950 pieces were struck in 1872, divided into 950 Proofs and 1,000 business strikes. Of the 950 Proofs minted, probably 500 or 600, some of them impaired, still exist today, for they were sold to collectors who paid a premium and saved them. Business strikes were not saved at the time of issue, and if one were to be auctioned today it would be recognized as an extreme rarity. Probably no more than a handful of Uncirculated (business strike) examples exist! This does not mean that a business strike would be tremendously expensive, for the demand for a top grade 1872 silver three-cent piece is easily satisfied by the more readily available Proofs. There aren't many collectors who have to have both a Proof and Uncirculated issue of the same date!

The Coinage Act of 1873 did many things—it added arrows to dimes, quarters, and half dollars alongside the dates of these pieces, it ended the coinage of the two-cent and half dime series, and among other provisions it also ended the silver-three cent pieces. So, this rather short-lived series, issued for a span of less than 25 years, came to an abrupt halt. The public did not miss these tiny, inconvenient pieces. Their popularity was not to come until nearly a century later, beginning in the early 1960s, when many collectors formed an intense interest in assembling type sets. Every such set of American coinage has to have one each of the silver three-cent piece designs, so in recent years the rush to obtain outstanding examples, particularly of the 1854-1858 years, has been frantic.

For the numismatist who wishes to form a complete collection by dates and major varieties, several possibilities are available. Issues from 1851 through 1862 are readily available in worn grades and exist in approximate proportion to original mintages. Issues after 1862 are seldom seen except in Proof or impaired Proof preservation. Thus, a "budget collection" of silver three-cent pieces could include Fine to Extremely Fine issues from 1851 through 1862, but dates from 1863 through 1873 would necessarily have to be in higher states of preservation. Although issues such as 1867, 1868, 1869, and other dates of the era posted nominal business strike or circulation mintages, in practice such coins are extreme rarities today. It is probably the case that *years* can elapse between offerings of a well-worn 1868 silver three-cent piece, although the value of such a coin is not apt to be great. For practical purposes, as noted, Proofs or impaired Proofs will have to be obtained.

If budget is not a consideration, then the deluxe way to go is to assemble a set of Proofs from 1858 (the first year such were sold to collectors) through 1873. Issues from 1851 through 1857 can be acquired in Uncirculated preservation. Hard to find in this grade will be 1851-O, 1854, 1855, 1856, and 1857, with 1856 being particularly rare. Examples of the Type II design in sharply struck Uncirculated condition will be nearly impossible to locate, so some compromise will be necessary in this regard. Scattered Proofs exist prior to 1858 and are major rarities and quite nice to acquire. However, they should not be insisted upon as a requirement for completion. Certain "Proofs" offered of earlier dates might not be Proofs at all. Occasionally, polished coins which have been heavily toned are offered as Proofs. If you are not sure of the coin, be sure of the dealer from whom you acquire it.

Beginning with a mintage of 50 Proofs in 1858, examples were sold to the general public. Mintages soon increased, and by 1860 a figure of 1,000 Proofs was posted. However, the Mint practice was to make such coins to put them "on the shelf," for *possible* sale to collectors. The true story is that many of them, sometimes substantial portions of the entire mintage, went to the melting pot. By 1862 Proof mintage had dwindled to just 550 pieces. This was due to two main reasons. First, the Mint realized the true demand and started producing pieces in quantities that were more realistic in view of actual sales. Second, during the middle of the Civil War the Mint posted a requirement that United States paper money could not be used to purchase coins! Indeed, coins sold at a premium in terms of paper money. So, it was necessary to pay for Proof coins by submitting the payment in other silver or gold coins, thus making it difficult to order such pieces easily.

In general, Proofs after the early 1860s, continuing through 1873, exist today in approximate proportion to the mintages. If, for example, one assumes that the mintage of 600 Proofs for 1869 is correct, then it is logical to estimate that perhaps a couple hundred were lost, strayed, or stolen and cannot be traced today, leaving, say, 400 pieces in numismatic hands. Of these pieces, in theory probably 100 to 200 (at most) are in grades that can be described as Proof-63 or Proof-65 (Select Proof or Choice Proof) today. The other 200 or so show impairment or cleaning. In particular, cleaning has been the great enemy of Uncirculated and Proof coins, commemorative coins, and other pieces which have attracted the attention of investors in recent decades. Many investors believe that "brilliant is best," with the result that a typical coin has made several trips through the coin cleaning process during the past 20 or 30 years. One dipping or cleaning might be fine, for such may simply transform a toned coin to a bright one, without ill effects. However, repeated dipping removes each time some metal from the coin's surface, finally resulting in a cloudy product.

Are you building a type set? Then you have three pieces to acquire among silver three-cent issues, one each of the Type I, II, and III designs. If you are building a set in circulated condition, then among Type I issues you can have your pick of 1851, 1852, or 1853. All are readily available, although the 1851 is slightly scarcer. 1851-O is scarcer yet and may be appealing as it is the only mintmark issue of the denomination. In Uncirculated condition you will find that 1851, 1852, and 1853 are readily available but, again, 1851 is slightly scarcer. 1851-O is very rare in strictly Uncirculated preservation.

Type II pieces are readily available in worn grades. Uncirculated issues are rare, and sharply struck Uncirculated pieces are exceedingly so. However, if your requirement is to have just one Type II silver three-cent piece of the 1854-1858 years, perhaps with some looking you can *eventually* acquire one which is both sharply struck and Uncirculated. It will require some patient hunting, however.

Type III pieces can be obtained in all grades. Worn examples from 1859 through 1862 are readily available. Although catalogues list such grades as Good and Very Good, these did not circulate to a great extent, so the average piece encountered is apt to be Fine or better. Uncirculated coins are available for the same dates, with 1861 and 1862 being those usually seen. As noted earlier, 1859, although it has a mintage higher than 1862, is much rarer—probably at least 50 times rarer in Uncirculated condition! Proofs of the Type III design are readily available. You might enjoy the satisfaction of having one of the low-mintage issues of the late 1860s or early 1870s. Typically, these cost little more than a Proof of the 1859-1862 years.

Collecting Nickel Five-Cent Pieces

1866 to Date

Shield Nickels

Nickel alloy five-cent pieces of the shield design first made their appearance in 1866. However, as a prelude to this, many different types of pattern coins were issued during the previous year, 1865, and earlier during the same year, 1866.

In the study of almost all coin denominations, patterns furnish an insight to "what might have been." It is often the case that many different designs, some quite artistically superior to those finally adopted, were tried before a particular style was first issued. In my opinion, the studies of pattern coins and regular issues are inseparable.

Early nickel five-cent piece patterns were made in many different styles. Among the most interesting are those with the portrait of President George Washington and other issues, rarities today, depicting President Abraham Lincoln.

The Shield nickel design as finally adopted is more of a geometric design than an artistic design. The devices are symmetrical on both sides, and there is little to recommend the piece as a work of art. It is more or less a copy of the shield on the two-cent piece issued earlier (in 1864). It seems to me that perhaps either the Washington or the Lincoln design would have been more interesting.

The first Shield nickel design regularly issued was the type with rays released in 1866. The obverse features the shield design, and the reverse depicts a circle of stars with radiant stripes or rays between them. Today collectors refer to this design as the "with rays" type, but 60 or 70 years ago this motif was designated as the "stars and bars" design in coin catalogues. The latter terminology has been largely forgotten today.

The term *nickel* came into use to designate this type of five-cent piece. As the composition is 7½ parts copper and 2½ parts nickel, the term *copper* would have been more appropriate! However, the relatively small amount of nickel gives the alloy a bright silver appearance, like nickel metal, so the term *nickel* stuck.

The initial year, 1866, saw a mintage of 14,742,500 pieces, with perhaps the tag-end 500 issued as Proofs. The type quickly caught on, and before long nickels were a staple in the channels of commerce, circulating alongside fractional currency notes, Indian cents, two-cent pieces, and nickel three-cent pieces. Silver coins were nowhere to be seen. Indeed, it was not until the mid-1870s that specie (coin) payments were resumed by the government, and Liberty Seated half dimes, quarters, and other issues were clinking in cash boxes.

The presence of rays or bars on the shield nickel caused some striking problems related to metal movement, so early in the year 1867, after 2,019,000 had been struck with the rays-type reverse, the rays were discontinued. Later in the year 28,890,500 of the new format were produced, thus isolating the 1867 with-rays nickel as a rare issue by comparison.

From the very outset problems with striking surfaced. The hard alloy caused rapid die wear. Metal movement was a problem. To prolong the life of dies and to facilitate striking, the obverse and reverse dies on the coining presses were spaced slightly farther apart than they might have otherwise been, with the result that light impressions characterize the majority of business strikes seen today. The die wear caused numerous breaks. With magnifying glass in hand, the interested numismatist can detect myriad traceries of breaks, usually along the border, on numerous early shield nickel issues. 1866 and 1867 seem to be particularly outstanding in this regard. To prolong their life, dies, once they became worn, were sometimes repunched in their entirety, but more often simply the date numerals were strengthened. This practice gave rise to many different varieties of date recuttings, again a situation particularly prevalent during the first few years of issue. For one die, the recutting was accomplished by severely misaligning the second set of 1867 numerals, thus creating a sharply doubled date. Another variety, this one of 1866, has a "ghost" earlier numeral 6, from a previous use of the die, visible after the regular 1866 date, giving the fanciful appearance of 18666.

Type set collectors have created an exceptional demand for pieces of the 1866 and 1867 type with-rays, with the result that these pieces, while not necessarily rarer than certain later dates, have commanded strong prices. The 1867 with-rays is a rarity, or at least a scarcity, on its own, but as most demand is from type set collectors, not date set collectors, in recent years the prices have become nearly identical. The market difference between an 1866 and an 1867 is very small.

The effect that type set collecting has had on the prices of certain early coins can be shown by many different examples. Illustrations pervade virtually every series. In brief, years ago, particularly before 1960 when type set collecting became popular, it did not make a great deal of difference whether an early design was short-lived or made for a long period of years. The basic or absolute rarity of the coin was more important. Whether it was rare *as a type* was not a major consideration. After 1960, when few numismatists could afford to collect "one of everything," figuratively speaking, type collecting became prominent. Suddenly, numismatists who were not collecting quarter dollars by dates wanted a 1796, simply because it was needed to illustrate the Draped Bust obverse and Small Eagle reverse, for this style was minted only in this single year. Rare dates diminished in importance. It was type that counted.

An interesting illustration of this is afforded by listings in *A Guide Book of United States Coins.* The 1954-1955 edition priced a Fine 1866 Shield nickel at $4 and an 1867 with-rays nickel in the same grade at $18. In other words, the 1867 with rays, being much rarer (about seven times rarer from mintage viewpoint), sold for 4½ times as much. Back then the demand was for pieces as types.

By contrast, the 1985 edition of the same publication priced a Fine 1866 at $20 and a Fine 1867 for $29, or only slightly more. A beneficial result of the present type set oriented market is that a collector with an eye to acquiring rarities can often obtain lower mintage or rarer issues at only slightly more than common ones, a sharp contrast to the situation faced by numismatists years ago. In a 1984 offering an 1882 Shield nickel in Choice Uncirculated grade was priced just ten percent less than a similarly-preserved 1871, although the 1871 is at least 50 times rarer!

From the standpoint of availability today, nickels of the 1866 and 1867 with-rays design can be obtained in all grades from Good through Uncirculated. In the latter grade 1867 with-rays is particularly elusive. Most pieces seen, particularly those dated 1866, are softly struck. Pieces with needle-sharp details are exceedingly elusive.

Proofs of 1866 are fairly scarce and may have been minted just to the extent of about 500 pieces (although the exact quantity has never been reported). Apparently sets sold to collectors early in the year, before the Shield nickel was introduced, lacked these coins. Today they are considered to be important issues. Proofs of the 1867 with rays are among the greatest of all American Proof rarities. Fewer than 20 are believed to exist.

The second design type in the Shield nickel series is furnished by the without rays style made from 1867 through 1883. Mintage was continuous throughout this span. Business strikes of several dates can be considered scarce, notably 1871 and, in particular, 1879 through 1881. Also elusive are two Proof-only issues, 1877 and 1878. In those two years no business strikes were produced.

Nearly all 1878 Proof nickels have a generous degree of "Uncirculated mint frost." In other words, they have lustrous, frosty surfaces like a

Obverse and reverse of an 1883 Shield nickel. Shown is the style minted from 1867 through 1883, without rays between the stars on the reverse.

business strike. Many show no traces of Proof surface whatever! It is an interesting debate whether pieces should be called Proofs because they were made that way by the Mint and sold as Proofs to collectors, or whether they should be called Uncirculated, for they appear to be in the latter grade. Tradition dictates the Proof classification.

At least two, possibly three, overdates occur within the series. Don Taxay lists an "1869/8" overdate in his *Comprehensive Catalogue and Encyclopedia of United States Coins*, but all such "overdates" seen by me have been recut dates and have not clearly shown an 8 under the 9. It is quite possible, however, that authentic overdates do indeed exist.

Very clearly recognizable overdates are the 1879/8, which occurs only in Proof condition (and which is about three times scarcer than a regular 1879 Proof), and the 1883/2. The latter overdate occurs in several die varieties, indicating that more than one die was overpunched. Confusing the situation of the 1883/2 overdate is the existence of a number of recut date 1883 Shield nickels which have one 1883 date punched over an earlier 1883 date, not over 1882. Still other regular 1883 Shield nickels show the final three "filled" and appearing more like a blob than a 3. This "blob" is particularly evident in specimens which have been slightly worn. Often these are sold as "1883/2," which they are not.

In Uncirculated grade, the most often seen date among Shield nickels of the 1867-1883 without rays type is the 1882, which also happens to be the highest mintage issue among later pieces. The frequency of circulated Shield nickels, from worn smooth through AU, is approximately proportional to the mintages, with 1867, 1868, and 1869 showing up especially often.

Proofs of later years in the series are readily available, although key dates such as 1877 and 1878 (Proof-only issues as no examples were made for circulation), and 1879 through 1881 tend to be more expensive. The latter years are not particularly rare in Proof grade, but business strikes are elusive, thus creating an additional demand for the Proofs.

SHIELD NICKELS

Shield nickels were produced from 1866 through 1883 inclusive. There are two major design types: the 1866-1867 type with rays on the reverse (a Proof rarity of which is shown above), and the 1867-1883 type without rays. Scarce dates in the shield nickel series, so far as business strikes are concerned, include 1867 with rays, 1871, 1879, 1880, and 1881. Among Proofs, the 1866 is rare, the 1867 with rays is extremely rare, and the 1877 and 1878 are Proof-only issues (that is, no 1877 or 1878 nickels were produced for circulation). It is believed that only about 500 examples of the 1877 were made.

LIBERTY NICKELS

Liberty nickels were produced from 1883 through 1913. The first year of issue, 1883, was made in two varieties, both of which are shown to the left. The first variety (shown at the bottom) does not bear the word CENTS and was confusing to the public. Issues produced from late 1883 through the end of the series included the word CENTS. Among regular issues, the scarcest dates are 1885 (a Proof example of which is shown above), 1886, and 1912-S. The 1913 Liberty nickel, of which just five are known, was produced unofficially to create a rarity for numismatists.

1883-1913 Liberty Head Nickels

Beginning in 1881, patterns were made for the so-called Liberty Head nickel design. The obverse featured a classic head of Miss Liberty, modeled after the goddess Diana it was said, a design which was considered at the time to be superior to the Shield motif. Liberty Head patterns were prepared of the one-cent, three-cent, and five-cent denominations. The value of each was stated in Roman numerals on the reverse, I, III, and V. No such standardization across these denominations was ever to take place, and the one-cent and three-cent pieces of this design were soon forgotten.

The Liberty Head motif lingered on for use with the nickel five-cent piece, and in 1882, many different patterns were produced. The obverse of most of these featured a head of Liberty surrounded by the legend UNITED STATES OF AMERICA. On the reverse the value was stated as V in combination with various wreaths and inscriptions. One piece, listed now as Judd-1690 in *United States Patterns*, is identical to the regular without-CENTS issue of the following year, 1883. This important transitional pattern has been a favorite with collectors. Around 1960 a specimen of this coin was displayed at one of the Central States Numismatic Society conventions. All by itself in solitary splendor the coin earned a prize! The 1882 Liberty nickel has great numismatic interest, just as the piece at the tail-end of the series, the 1913 Liberty nickel, does.

In 1883 the issuing of patterns continued. Particularly interesting among Liberty Head patterns of this year are those with different metallic compositions. Some pieces were made in pure nickel. As the difference between pure nickel and various nickel alloys was not discernible to the unaided eye the Mint did a logical thing: it lettered the metallic composition on the reverse of the coin as part of the design. Hence, those struck in pure nickel have the bold lettering PURE NICKEL across the reverse. Pieces struck in 75 parts nickel and 25 parts copper have that particular formula as part of the design, and pieces which consist of 50 parts copper and 50 parts nickel are likewise so designated.

Still another variety is provided by examples consisting of 33 parts nickel and 67 parts copper.

All of this is well and fine, except that these dies were also used to strike coins in metal alloys other than those intended! The numismatist today can puzzle over the anomalous situation in which the aforementioned pure nickel design (listed as Judd-1704) was struck not only in pure nickel (which can be identified by being readily attracted to a magnet), but also in nickel alloy (non-magnetic), and aluminum!

Before leaving the subject of pattern nickels, several other interesting issues were produced in the same era. In 1884 and 1885 nickels with holes in the center were made, a format perhaps borrowed from Chinese coins. In 1896 a new type of "Shield nickel" was made in pattern form.

In 1883 the first regular Liberty nickels were made for circulation. The earliest design bore as a denomination the large letter V on the reverse. The word CENTS was not present. No one at the Mint gave any thought to a potential problem, for the pieces looked like nickels and were the size and shape of the then-familiar Shield types. However, the Mint did not reckon with the ingenuity of American citizens.

No sooner did the new Liberty nickels without CENTS appear than an interesting type of fraud was perpetrated with them. Certain individuals gold plated the new nickels, and some with machining facilities even added reeded edges. As the diameter of the nickel is approximately the same as that of the United States $5 gold piece, a gold-plated Liberty nickel could be mistaken for a $5 gold piece of a new design. At this time the Liberty nickel design was not familiar to the public as a design for nickels, so anyone seeing such a gold plated piece had no reason to attribute it to a lower value. The numeral V on the reverse, of course, could equally stand for $5 or 5c.

Gold-plated 1883 without-CENTS nickels were evidently made in large quantities, for specimens are often seen today with traces of gold plating made years ago. The story of these pieces, often called "racketeer nickels" today, has been recounted numerous times in numismatic literature. It has been related that one of the favorite ways to pass such pieces back in 1883 was not to offer one and say, "Here is a five-dollar gold piece, please give me change," but, rather, to purchase something such as a cigar or a piece of candy with a value of one or two cents. The 1883 Liberty nickel plated to resemble a $5 gold piece would be tendered in payment. No words would be said. If the shopkeeper then gave $4.98 in change for a two-cent purchase, then the deception was complete. But, for legal purposes the person spending the nickel had not stated that it was a $5 gold piece so could claim complete innocence in the matter! On the other hand, should the shopkeeper return only three cents, realizing that it was a nickel that had been offered, then the owner of the nickel could ask for that coin back and give him another one which had not been gold plated.

The Mint soon realized that it had made a mistake in the design. So, later in the year 1883 the word CENTS was added to the reverse. From 1883 through 1913 the design remained this style.

News of the Mint's oversight spread rapidly, and it was said that all of the error nickels without CENTS would be recalled. This precipitated a wild scramble, and vast quantities were squirreled away in bureau drawers, toy banks, and other locations. Feeding on this untrue rumor, sellers of coins and curiosities found a ready profit could be turned by selling such pieces to speculators and investors. As late as October 1886, long after the hoarding fervor had passed, John M. Hubbard, an early coin and stamp dealer, ran the following notice:

"The government has been calling in the V nickels of 1883 without CENTS ever since their coinage was stopped. They are melted and coined into the common nickels. We have a few of the variety without CENTS which we are selling at 15c each. Everyone who does not own a specimen should procure one at once as in a short time they will cost much more."

Eventually 1883 without-CENTS nickels purchased at three times face value in 1886 proved to be good investments, but not until more than a half century later. As recently as the 1940s, specimens traded hands in bulk quantities at just slightly over face value. With the advent of the popularity of type set collecting around 1960, the 1883 without-CENTS nickel became the object of desire for thousands of new buyers, for such a coin was absolutely necessary to complete a grouping of nickels by designs. Year by year the price rose as the demand increased. Today large quantities are seldom seen, and Choice Uncirculated individual specimens are highly desired.

As numismatists were also caught up in the desire to own 1883 Liberty nickels without the CENTS feature, the Mint made 5,219 Proofs, one of the highest Proof mintage figures ever. Apparently many of the nickels were sold in sets, for large numbers of 1883 Proof shield nickels and Liberty nickels with CENTS were also produced.

Today the 1883 Liberty nickel without CENTS is the most plentiful Liberty nickel in grades above Very Fine. Specimens are easily obtained and demand for them is widespread.

Following the addition of CENTS later in 1883, nickels continued to be struck with this design through the year 1913. A number of scarce and rare issues exist within the series. 1885, with a business strike mintage of 1,476,490, is one of the most elusive, particularly in Uncirculated grade, for few were saved (collectors at the time preferred Proofs). 1886 is also scarce, as is 1894. While worn specimens of Liberty nickels exist in approximate proportion to the mintage figures, Uncirculated issues survived only as a matter of chance and are not available with the same consistency. Abe Kosoff once told me that he spent several *years* looking for an Uncirculated 1891 Liberty nickel for a customer. His client insisted on an Uncirculated piece; a Proof wouldn't do. Finally he located an example. Equipped with this knowledge I set about looking for 1891 Uncirculated nickels on my own, and while the issue seemed to be scarce, I was able to buy several over a period of years. This goes to show that what might be difficult for one person to locate might be acquired easily by another. Still, in terms of absolute supplies, an Uncirculated 1891 nickel is definitely rare, as are many other issues of the late nineteenth century. Most often seen today in Uncirculated grade are pieces from the late 1890s through 1912.

In the latter year nickels were struck at branch mints for the first time. The 1912-D nickel made its appearance as did the 1912-S, the latter with a restricted mintage of just 238,000. Immediately the 1912-S became scarce, and since the time of issue it has been considered to be a key date. Examples were struck from a bulged obverse die, with the result that the fields on a 1912-S nickel are slightly curved or bulged, quite unlike any other nickel in the series. This characteristic makes it easy to pinpoint when an S mintmark has been fraudulently added to a regular 1912 Philadelphia issue.

Diebreaks are often seen among early Liberty nickels, with issues of 1883 and 1884 being particularly plentiful in this regard. Uncirculated pieces of all dates are apt to show light striking on several obverse stars or at the lower part of the wreath on the reverse.

Proofs were made of all varieties from 1883 through 1912. Two interesting variations among Proofs may be of interest to nickel collectors. The first is a variety of the 1883 without-CENTS on which the S of PLURIBUS is sharply doubled. Normally a recut letter does not attract much attention, but in this instance it is interesting to note that the same reverse die was used to make the transitional pattern 1882 Liberty nickel. The recut letter, which is sharply visible under magnification, serves as an identifying feature. Perhaps one out of three or four 1883 Proof nickels of this type has this recutting.

During the production of 1903 Liberty nickels at the Mint someone made a glaring mistake. During the striking of some pieces, the dies, rather than being oriented 180 degrees apart (so that the reverse appears upside-down), were aligned in the same direction. Of the total mintage of 1,790 Proof nickels of the year it is doubtful that more than a couple hundred had this slip. This issue, which has been overlooked by most cataloguers, first came to my attention around 1961 when my firm acquired the beautiful collection of coins formed by Ambrose

Brown of Penn Yan, New York. His set of Proof Liberty nickels was mounted in a type of holder in which both sides of each coin are visible. Upon looking at the reverses I noticed that one was upside-down in relation to the others. I immediately thought that the coin had been placed in the holder upside-down, but upon examining the obverses of all the pieces I found that they were aligned properly. Ever since that time I have been on the lookout for 1903 Proof Liberty nickels with inverted reverses, and I have seen perhaps a dozen examples.

The rarity of Proof Liberty nickels is not particularly related to the rarity of Uncirculated Liberty nickels. As an example, 1,475 Proofs were made in 1907 as compared to more than 39 million business strikes. The Proof mintage ranks the 1907 as the rarest Proof in the series, while the generous business strike mintage reflects the situation that specimens in grades up to and including Uncirculated are among the most plentiful of the later dates. On the other hand, 1885, a prime scarcity in Uncirculated condition, is not particularly elusive in Proof, for 3,790 were struck in the latter format.

The last coin in the Liberty nickel series, the 1913, is a story in itself. In 1972 the *Numismatic Scrapbook Magazine* ran a fascinating feature article written by Courtney Coffing. The text delved into every aspect of this famous issue: how it was made, how it was publicized, the history of specimens trading over the years, and the collections possessing them. The story is one of the most absorbing I have ever read.

Not an official mint issue, the 1913 Liberty Head nickel was made privately at the Philadelphia Mint, presumably by one or more employees there (and also presumably without the knowledge of the officials of that institution). Samuel W. Brown, who supervised the security of the dies but who later moved to North Tonawanda, New York, to serve as mayor (and who later achieved minor publicity as a coin collector), has been pinpointed as the likely originator. At the time of issue the existence of the 1913 Liberty nickel was known only to the person or persons who made them. It was not until 1919 that Brown ran advertisements in *The Numismatist* seeking to *buy* such pieces, as if he knew they existed. Then, magically, at the 1920 ANA convention he appeared with a display of five of them! The implication, of course, was that he had bought them through his advertisements, but in later years when it was disclosed that he worked at the Mint in the coining department in 1913, a situation generally unknown to collectors in 1920, his source became suspect. Since no others have come to light since 1920, it is presumed that just five were struck, but the true story probably never will be known.

The 1913 Liberty nickel achieved fantastic fame during the 1920s and 1930s when B. Max Mehl used it as a focal point of his advertising to sell copies of his *Star Rare Coin Encyclopedia*, a compact volume which discussed all types of coins and listed the prices Mehl would pay for them. He spent hundreds of thousands of dollars yearly advertising in magazines, newspapers, Sunday supplements, and even on the radio. Millions of citizens looked at their change hoping to find a rare 1913 Liberty nickel. None did. Thus, the coin became a household word with the American public.

Whenever a 1913 Liberty nickel changes hands publicly it is a matter of great interest to collectors and dealers. The J.V. McDermott specimen of this coin, bought by Aubrey Bebee for $46,000 at the American Numismatic Association convention in 1967, made headlines as did the purchase by World Wide Coin Company of the Edwin Hydeman coin from dealer Abe Kosoff. The latter specimen was handled by my firm, and through another company, Superior Galleries, was sold into the Jerry Buss collection. Another example, for which my firm provided an appraisal, was donated by Hon. and Mrs. R. Henry Norweb to the Smithsonian Institution in 1982. The Jerry Buss specimen was scheduled to cross the auction block in January 1985, shortly after this book went to press.

While owning a 1913 Liberty nickel is the stuff of which dreams are made, and few will ever have that opportunity, the assembling of a set of regular issue Liberty nickels from 1883 to 1912 is a realistic goal. The most elusive issues are 1885 and 1912-S, followed by 1886. For those who can afford it, a run of Proofs, plus Uncirculated examples of 1912-D and 1912-S, forms a nice set. Much more difficult to piece together, but less expensive, is a run of Uncirculated pieces from 1883 onward.

In my opinion the Liberty nickel is one of the most attractive coin designs used for circulation during the past century. To me the coin seems to have an interesting sense of "Americana" about it, somewhat as the Indian cent does. Perhaps it is because so many Liberty nickels were made and because they were widely used by the public. Perhaps it is because the 1913 Liberty nickel has drawn attention to the series as a whole. The hypothetical travels of a worn Liberty nickel form the basis for the chapter, "Nickeldom," in my book *Adventures with Rare Coins*.

One of the most famous of the five known 1913 Liberty nickels is the Hydeman specimen shown above. It passed to World-Wide Coin Company, then to the author's firm, then to Dr. Jerry Buss, through Superior Galleries. As this present book went to press the nickel was scheduled to cross the auction block once again in the sale of the Buss Collection in January 1985.

Last Minute News: On January 28, 1985, Superior Galleries sold the Buss 1913 Liberty nickel for $385,000 to a Texas numismatist.

ABOVE: B. Max Mehl, the noted Texas dealer, is shown in his private office circa 1930. A promoter extraordinaire, Mehl had every school boy in America looking for prized 1913 Liberty nickel, for which he offered to pay $500 (see next page).

LEFT: Cover of "The Star Rare Coin Encyclopedia," issued by Mehl at $1. Listed were buying prices for various U.S. and other coins.

NUMISMATIC COMPANY OF TEXAS 21

United States Nickel Coins

NICKEL THREE-CENT PIECES

Coined at the Philadelphia mint only.
Coinage commenced in 1865, discontinued in 1889.

1865 to 1876, each	$ .05 to $ .25
1877	5.00 to 10.00
1878	1.00 to 3.00
1879 to 1889, each	.10 to 1.00

"NICKELS" OR FIVE-CENT PIECES

Coined at the Philadelphia, Denver and San Francisco mints.
Coinage commenced in 1866.

1866	$ .10 to $ 1.00
1867	.20 to 1.25
1868 to 1870	.10 to 1.00
1871	.50 to 3.00
1872 to 1876	.25 to 1.00
1877	5.00 to 10.00
1878	1.00 to 3.00
1879 to 1884	.10 to 1.00
1885	2.00 to 10.00
1886 to 1898	.10 to 1.00
1899 to 1912	.05 to 1.00
1912 D. Mint	.05 to 3.00
1912 S. Mint	1.00 to 5.00

The Famous 1913 Liberty Head 5c Nickel

1913 With LIBERTY HEAD (not Buffalo Type)......$500.00

BUFFALO TYPE 5c NICKELS

1913 to 1938	$ .05 to $ .50
1913 D. Mint	.05 to 2.00

A page from "The Star Rare Coin Encyclopedia" notes that B. Max Mehl would pay $500 for the rare 1913 Liberty Head nickel—a coin he used prominently in his advertising.

B. Max Mehl, who is more closely identified with the 1913 Liberty nickel than any other person, was an innovative advertiser. In this 1940 message he pointed out that Fort Worth, Texas was close to just about anywhere by air, a relatively new method of commercial travel at the time.

THE 1913 LIBERTY NICKEL AT AUCTION

A 1913 Liberty Nickel Sells at Auction in 1967

Note: The following is a transcript of an interview conducted by Donn Pearlman, well-known CBS radio personality, with Aubrey and Adeline Bebee. The interview took place in 1984 and relates to an exciting event at the earlier convention of the American Numismatic Association in Miami in 1967. The auction for that convention, catalogued by Paramount International Coin Corporation, featured the J.V. McDermott example of the famous 1913 Liberty nickel.

* * *

PEARLMAN: When you went into the auction in Miami were you determined to say "That coin is going to be mine!"? What was your thinking about it?

BEBEE: I was hopeful of being the successful bidder in that auction. We were attending a Society of Paper Money Collectors banquet and when the speakers came on I said to my wife, "Honey, I'm going to go over to the auction to see them auction off this 1913 nickel." She had no idea I was going to try and buy it!

PEARLMAN: If she had known, would you still have been able to buy it that night?

BEBEE: Well,...

PEARLMAN: Adeline is shaking her head no...

BEBEE: I believe so (laughter). When I arrived there (the auction room), I walked up to the auctioneer, James Kelly (the late prominent dealer from Dayton, Ohio who owned in 1942 and 1943 three of the five 1913 Liberty nickels), and said: "Jim, what kind of a price do you think this nickel might bring?" He said, "Oh, maybe $38,000." I said, "Jim, I'm willing to go $52,000 or more on the nickel." There's not many dealers that I would give that information to, of course. So, when they came to that lot, Jim Kelly announced: "We're now going to auction off the 1931 nickel!" And, everyone laughed, and then he corrected himself, (saying) "1913 Liberty Head nickel."

The nickel started at $40,000, opening bid. Someone bid 41 and I went to 42. Then 43, then I bid 44, someone bid 45, and I bid 46 and was the successful buyer.

Standing in the wings was Abe Kosoff (a prominent New York and later California dealer who personally bought and sold most of the great U.S. numismatic rarities before his death in 1983) with one of the Dupont family members who was a famous collector. He could have gone to $100,000 if he wanted to, but when we hit $46,000 he shook his head to Abe and said, "No, we're not interested." So, we walked away with the $46,000 nickel.

PEARLMAN: And then what happened? Someone offered you a $10,000 profit soon after that?

BEBEE: Yes, there was a collector, P.B. Trotter, Jr., an executive of the Union Planters Bank, from Memphis, Tennessee who came to the auction purposely to buy the nickel. But there was one hour's difference in time (between Memphis and Miami), and he set his watch the wrong way. So, when he came in and he said, "Aubrey, I understand you got the nickel. I'll give you a $10,000 profit for it if you want to sell it right away." I said, "No," and he said, "Well, how about $12,000?" I said, "No, it's not for sale." We've had the nickel ever since.

PEARLMAN: Two instances of fate and circumstance. Someone setting his clock the wrong way and getting to the auction too late, and someone who could afford the nickel, from the Dupont family, deciding not to buy it.

BEBEE: Yeah, that's right. And, it was quite an eventful sale.

Aubrey E. Bebee proudly displays the J.V. McDermott specimen of the 1913 Liberty Head nickel which he purchased at auction for $46,000 at the American Numismatic Association convention sale held in 1966 by Paramount International Coin Corporation. Later, the coin was exhibited many places and brought the owner much acclaim.

PEARLMAN: Another thing, you have always been so generous in carrying on the tradition that (James) McDermott (of Milwaukee who purchased that particular 1913 Liberty nickel specimen for $900 from James F. Kelly in 1943) had of exhibiting the nickel, of letting people see it and not just keeping it in a safe, secure vault somewhere. You've shown it at various coin shows and had it on display at the 1979 American Numismatic Association convention in St. Louis (at a cost to Bebee of $2,000 to transport the coin by armed guard to the show and back to his Omaha bank). That must bring you a lot of personal satisfaction to be able to share it.

BEBEE: Yes, it really does. So many people will walk up and say, "Well, I was standing there when you bought the nickel (laughter)!"

After the auction, there must have been a dozen people who said, "Come over here, I want you to stand by me while they snap my picture (more laughter)!"

PEARLMAN: Adeline Bebee, you were shaking your head "No" before. If you had known Aubrey was going to buy the nickel and go to the $46,000, would he be the owner of the nickel today?

MRS. BEBEE: Not if I had anything to say about it, no (laughter)! I was scared. I really didn't want it because of the publicity, mainly, you know. There was a lot of publicity. But I'm really happy he bought it—now.

PEARLMAN; It's brought you a lot of joy in sharing it.

MRS. BEBEE: Yes, it really has. You know, we're pretty proud to own it, really.

PEARLMAN; Thank you, both. I appreciate your sharing the story.

Two footnotes: Two years after Bebee purchased the famous coin at the 1967 ANA convention in Miami, the same Memphis collector who offered Bebee an immediate $12,000 profit raised the ante. At the 1969 ANA Philadelphia convention, the prominent collector offered Bebee $75,000, but was politely turned down.

Also, Adeline Bebee's concern and prediction about publicity quickly became reality. When she and her husband returned to Omaha from the Miami convention she thought no one yet knew about their historic purchase. However, the next morning, when they arrived at their coin shop (then located at 4514 North 30th Street) several reporters and photographers already were waiting for them!

In Illinois the Coin and Stamp Department of a Sears & Roebuck store featured "The 1913 Liberty Head Nickel for Your Viewing."

Store visitors examine the prized 1913 Liberty nickel. Perhaps more so than any other American numismatic rarity, the 1913 Liberty nickel has attracted wide public attention in recent decades. (Photographs on this page courtesy of Donn Pearlman)

1913-1938 Buffalo Nickels

In 1913 a new nickel design appeared, the Indian or buffalo style. Although reference books sometimes call these "Indian head nickels," nearly all numismatists as well as citizens in general prefer the "buffalo nickel" term. Perhaps the "Indian" designation is special and is reserved for Indian cents. The nomenclature is further confused by the fact that the creature on the reverse of this particular design is not a buffalo at all but, properly speaking, is a bison. Presumably zoologists know the difference, but most numismatists could care less!

The obverse bears a realistic portrait of an Indian modeled by sculptor James E. Fraser, who used three different Indians to create a composite. The bison on the reverse is a likeness of Black Diamond, who resided for many years in a New York zoo.

Buffalo nickels are of two main varieties, usually referred to as Type I and Type II. Both are necessary to complete a type set. The first style was coined only at the beginning of 1913 and features the buffalo (I defer to popular usage, *bison* would seem strange) on a raised mound. Soon apparent was the fact that the design would wear too quickly, so it was revised to portray the buffalo on a plain. The words FIVE CENTS, formerly in prominent relief on the mound, were relocated to a more protected position below the line formed by the plain.

Buffalo nickels were made from 1913 through 1938 inclusive. In contrast to the Shield and Liberty styles of an earlier era, Buffalo nickels are more like a medal than a coin. There is very little "field" or flat area on either the obverse or the reverse. The coins are almost sculpted in appearance.

A number of interesting scarcities and varieties occur throughout the series. As noted, 1913 was made in two types. Specimens of each were struck at Philadelphia, Denver, and San Francisco. The 1913-S Type II is viewed as particularly elusive.

Matte Proofs were made at the Philadelphia Mint from 1913 through 1916. Like Matte Proof Lincoln cents, these were unpopular with collectors, most of whom preferred the earlier "brilliant" or mirrorlike sur-

Models, reversed, by James E. Fraser. These models, dated 1912, were early experiments leading to the Buffalo nickel design eventually adopted in 1913.

faces. Proofs were again coined in 1936 and 1937, and these were of the brilliant finish with polished fields. However, some of those produced early in 1936 are only partially polished and appear to be hybrid between a business strike and a Proof.

A variety of 1916 occurs with a sharply doubled date. 1918/7-D is the only overdate in the series and is scarce in all grades, with Uncirculated examples being major rarities.

The high relief of the Buffalo design combined with the hardness of nickel metal made striking a problem. As a result, well struck pieces are the exception rather than rule. Particularly among Denver and San Francisco mint issues from 1914 through 1931, examples nearly always are lightly impressed in certain portions. The most obvious illustration is provided by the 1926-D, a coin which nearly always is indistinct. A piece freshly ejected from the coining press had no more detail than if it had been in circulation for 20 years! However, a few sharply struck 1926-D nickels exist and are great rarities.

The collector assembling a set of Buffalo nickels soon learns what reasonable expectations are regarding sharpness of details. The building of a completely sharply struck set of nickels from 1913 to 1938 may not be a *theoretical* impossibility, but considering the life span and patience of the average collector, it is a *practical* impossibility. I have never seen it done!

In Uncirculated condition and the various gradations thereof, most Denver and San Francisco issues of the 'teens and 'twenties are quite rare, and catalogue values reflect this. A number of clever forgeries have been made by a rather complicated process: by drilling a hole in the edge of a Philadelphia Mint coin, creating a recess below where the S or D mintmark location would be on a branch mint coin, and then pressing or embossing such an S or D by applying pressure from within the coin. The hole on the edge is later sealed, rendering detection difficult. As is the case with any rare coin, the best protection for authenticity is to buy from an established dealer who guarantees his merchandise. Fabrications are not bargains at any price. Another interesting sham has been conducted from time to time by nickel-plating worn specimens of Buffalo nickels, thus giving them a bright appearance. However, the surfaces are not quite correct and the edges differ on such pieces. A few years ago an "Uncirculated" 1918/7-D nickel advertised at a bargain price proved to be a Very Fine example which had been plated!

The final years of the Buffalo nickel provided two interesting varieties. The 1937-D "three legged" issue has the foreleg of the buffalo missing. This was not caused by an error in design but was due to detail lost when the reverse die was ground down to make it useful

Enlarged illustration of a 1913 Type I Buffalo nickel featuring the buffalo on a raised mound on the reverse. Later issues had the buffalo on a flat surface.

for coinage after it had been damaged by "clashing" with the obverse die—when both dies came together without a planchet in between them.

The 1938-D/S "overmintmark" nickel is particularly fascinating. Discovered shortly after 1960, the knowledge of this piece created a sensation among numismatists. Never before had anyone even fantasized that a coin would show two different mintmarks, one over the other. Collectors took out their magnifying glasses, and in the years since then several similar issues have come to light in various series.

What evidently happened is this: Dies for use in the branch mints, Denver and San Francisco, are all prepared at the Philadelphia facility. Those intended for use in San Francisco have "S" mintmarks punched into the die, and those for use in Denver have "D" letters added. In 1938 the Buffalo design was discontinued. However, coinage was still going on early in the year at the Denver mint, but no examples were made at San Francisco or Philadelphia. Apparently early in 1938 the people preparing dies knew that no further coinage of the Buffalo design would occur in San Francisco. On hand were two Buffalo nickel reverse dies with San Francisco mintmarks. What should be done with them? There were two possibilities: The dies could be discarded (which would result in slight waste) or they could be saved for use by heavily punching a D mintmark over the S. The latter situation is what occurred, and thus the 1938-D/S nickel (which occurs in two minutely different varieties, indicating that at least two reverse dies were prepared in this manner) was created.

Why wasn't the 1938-D/S, an overmintmark which is glaringly obvious even with a low power glass, discovered earlier? This is a question that was asked many times during the early 1960s when the variety first came to light. Perhaps the most obvious answer is that 1938-D Buffalo nickels were and still are rather common, and no one gave any attention to studying them. As is the case of the famous Purloined Letter story, sometimes the most obvious place provides the most interesting possibilities!

Buffalo nickels of the 1930s are fairly plentiful in all grades. Quantities of Uncirculated pieces were saved of issues after 1934, and occasional groups or rolls of such issues as 1930-S, 1931-S, 1934, and 1934-D are seen, as are quantities of most other issues of the 1930s.

For the collector interested in assembling a set of date and mintmark varieties, a condition expectation of Extremely Fine to AU for issues from 1913 through 1929 (although 1913 Type I is readily available in Uncirculated grade) is reasonable, with the balance of the set from 1930 onward in Uncirculated preservation. Budget permitting, trying for a complete Uncirculated set is a real challenge, but, as always, it is important to be realistic about expectations for sharpness among Denver and San Francisco coins.

Following the discontinuation of the Buffalo nickel in 1938, specimens remained in circulation for many years. Even as recently as the 1950s it was possible to fill many spaces in an album simply by looking through pocket change. Today they have all but disappeared.

1938 to Date Jefferson Nickels

Jefferson nickels, still being minted today, were first coined in 1938. The design represents the work of Felix O. Schlag, an independent artist who entered a national competition with approximately 390 others and who won a monetary award of $1,000 plus the intangible benefit of seeing his design produced on billions of coins. The obverse portrays a handsome bust of President Jefferson. The reverse depicts Jefferson's home, Monticello, located in Charlottesville, Virginia. The original Schlag design showed a view of the building from a corner, but the finished result is a plan view or head-on depiction. The dome of Monticello is bare—that is, it does not have a flagpole. When these nickels were first released it was reported that the Mint had made an error and that nickels without flagpoles would become valuable. Billions of coins later, Monticello still has no flagpole!

Specimens were coined from the outset at Philadelphia, Denver, and San Francisco. In 1942, due to wartime demands for nickel metal, a special alloy of copper, silver, and manganese was produced for five-cent piece coinage. It was realized at the time that in some future date it would be necessary to separate these special-alloy coins from others when worn pieces were turned into the Treasury for reclamation. This separation was necessary in order to more easily melt down the pieces and separate the various metals. To aid in this future recovery, mintmarks, including a large P for Philadelphia (representing the first time that such an initial was ever used to represent that mint), were placed above Monticello on the reverse. These pieces, which were nicknamed "wartime nickels" (by Harry Forman, I believe), were made from 1942 through 1945. Uncirculated examples have a particularly brilliant, lustrous, and frosty appearance due to the silver content. However, worn examples are duller than those made from nickel alloy. Sometimes the wartime issues are collected separately as sets.

An interesting variety of 1944 nickels made the news a number of years ago. Some enterprising counterfeiters decided to make coins of this date. Unfortunately, they didn't have a copy of *A Guide Book of*

United States Coins, nor did they know anything about coins. To create the obverse die they copied a 1944 nickel. For the reverse die they copied a Philadelphia Mint nickel of some other date, but not one of the wartime issues. In any event, unlike real 1944 nickels produced by the Philadelphia Mint, which bore a large "P" mintmark over the dome of Monticello, the counterfeits had no mintmark at all. When first released in circulation these were sighted by numismatists and deemed peculiar, an event which led to the capture and arrest of the counterfeiters!

In 1946 the coinage of regular nickels of the usual alloy (7½ parts copper and 2½ parts nickel) was resumed. In 1966 a minor change was made by adding the letters FS, the first and last initials of Felix O. Schlag, on the obverse of the coin. Agitation by *Coin World* and by columnist Mort Reed was largely responsible for this long-overdue recognition of Schlag's 1938 accomplishment. The artist, however, stated that he would have preferred use of his full initials, FOS.

In 1968 another change occurred. The mintmark position was moved from the back of the coin to the front. All branch mint issues since 1968 feature a letter below the date.

A number of interesting varieties occur in the Jefferson nickel series. Certain 1939 pieces exist with the words MONTICELLO and FIVE CENTS sharply doubled, a phenomenon similar to that on the 1955 Doubled Die cent. This was caused by a shift in the hub die in the preparation of the coining die. Specimens of this variety are fairly scarce, but as they have not been publicized they are not particularly expensive. The writer once bought several dozen worn specimens from Malcolm O.E. Chell-Frost, an old-time Boston dealer. Uncirculated examples are rarities.

Overmintmarks exist for 1949-D/S, 1954-S/D, and 1955-D/S. These are fairly scarce, but as popular albums do not have openings for them, they are not in great demand (and, thus, are relatively inexpensive).

While some specialists delve into overmintmarks or seek the 1943/2-P (which was discovered in recent years), most collectors endeavor to own one each of the standard date and mintmark issues. Several are scarce. As might be expected, issues of 1938, the first year, were saved in somewhat larger numbers due to the novelty of the design and, to a lesser extent, to the rumor of the flagpole error. Among early issues 1939-D is the scarcest and has always been considered the key date. 1939-S is elusive in Mint State. The 1942-D nickel struck in regular (not wartime) alloy is likewise scarce in Uncirculated grade.

The most famous of all Jefferson nickel "rarities" is the 1950-D. When Mint reports indicated that just 2,630,030 nickels were made of that issue, a figure far lower than for any other in the series, a wild scram-

Enlarged illustration of a 1939-D Jefferson nickel, an issue considered to be a key date in the series.

ble commenced. A number of dealers and collectors, notably A.J. Mitula of Texas, succeeded in acquiring large quantities before they were released into circulation. The price of $2 for a roll of 40 coins quickly jumped to $6, then to $10, then to far more. At one time (around 1964) rolls sold for as much as $1,200. Later the fever subsided. A.J. Mitula maintained a summer place in Cascade, Colorado, on the slopes of Pikes Peak. He was fond of calling it "the house that 1950-D nickels built." The 1950-D nickel indeed proved to be rare in circulation. Today worn pieces are seen less often than are Uncirculated coins.

Collecting Jefferson nickels by dates and mintmarks has been a popular pursuit for many. Interestingly, the price of a complete set moved relatively little from the early 1960s through the next two decades. Coin prices tend to follow cycles, and when values are doubling, tripling, or quadrupling in some other series, prices in another area may trend upward only slightly. Then the order of things changes, and a previously "hot" area cools off, and a dormant series has its day in the sun.

Some numismatists have made a specialty of Jefferson nickels. Those interested in going into the field more than just casually may want to investigate obtaining a strong magnifying glass with the object of seeking as many sharply struck pieces as possible. The steps on Monticello on the reverse have usually been designated as the benchmark for determining striking sharpness. Coins designated as "full steps" have all of the parallel step lines sharply visible.

The wartime series of nickels from 1942 through 1945, the issues struck in silver alloy with mintmarks above the dome, are for the most part readily available with full steps. The wartime alloy was softer and easier to strike than the normal nickel alloy, so metal flowed more readily, and the deepest recesses in the die were filled completely. Further, with this alloy the dies were less subject to wear and remained sharp for a longer period of time. 1944-S and 1945-S are scarce with full steps, however.

Considering the rest of the series, issues struck in regular nickel alloy, many variations can be found. 1939 (Philadelphia) nickels are common in Uncirculated grade, but with full steps they are relatively elusive. Other early issues which are scarce to relatively rare with full steps include 1939-S, 1940-S, 1941-S, and most other San Francisco coins through 1954.

In the Jefferson nickel series it seems that the later the date, the more sloppy the strike. Perhaps this was caused by the diminished purchasing power of the nickel, the vastly increased quantities of production, and emphasis on government economy (keeping worn dies in use for a longer period of time). 1952 Philadelphia issues, even those taken from original rolls, are apt to have dark purplish or brown surfaces with many marks. As if this were not enough, the strikes are likewise usually poor. Philadelphia Mint nickels of 1953, 1954, and 1955 often display wear characteristics as do those of 1957 and 1958. 1962-D is rare with full sharp striking and minimal bagmarks. Bernard Nagengast, a student of the series, observed in 1982 that sharply-struck 1962-D nickels commanded prices as high as $175 (at a time when a normal Uncirculated coin was worth a half dollar or less!). In sharply struck condition the 1963-D, 1964-D, 1968-D, 1969-D, and 1970-D are likewise elusive for the specialist. Just as some large cent collectors couldn't care less about attributing cents of 1851 or 1852 to specialized varieties listed in the Newcomb reference, many collectors of modern issues could care less whether Monticello has five steps, three, or none at all. However, for those who do care, such "magnifying glass collecting" can be a challenging pursuit. In the late 1950s one of our clients, Warren Snow, used to spend countless hours looking through rolls of Jefferson nickels to find one that was "just right" from a striking viewpoint. He was marching virtually alone at the time, for few others even knew about such things. Now many hear the same drumbeat.

In a letter dated January 1, 1984, Bernard Nagengast, whose publication *The Jefferson Nickel Analyst* has achieved wide recognition, wrote to me as follows:

> "As for 'full step' rarity, the ten rarest issues in MS-63 or better condition, fully struck with five or more steps, by actual appearance observed in the market are: 1953-S (unknown so far), 1969-D (unknown so far), 1960-D (fewer than five known), 1961-D (fewer than five known), and the following varieties of which fewer than ten are known of each: 1954-S, 1962-D, 1963-D, 1964-D, 1968-D, and 1970-D."
>
> Continuing, Mr. Nagengast noted: "This list does not include overmintmark varieties. To date, no one to my knowledge has completed the Jefferson nickel series from 1938 onward in MS-63 or better grade, with each coin having full steps and full strike."

As a series, Jefferson nickels have much to offer. As noted, they can be collected casually by date and mintmark or technically by overmintmarks and full steps to Monticello. Either way, the series comprises dozens of different issues with a relatively low total cost.

THE STORY BEHIND THE JEFFERSON NICKEL

By Felix O. Schlag

Note: The following is a transcript of an address given by Felix O. Schlag in 1964 at the American Numismatic Association Convention. The transcript was furnished by Margo Russell, Beth Deisher, and Dorothy Cernyar of "Coin World."

Twenty six years ago an American numismatic event moved me in the spotlight for a short time. It is the general opinion that it made me rich and famous.

Recently, Jefferson nickel collectors have taken me out of the mothballs, and I must admit that I enjoy it and am glad to be at this convention.

The story of the Jefferson nickel has interwoven in it many personal and human elements. In order to impress upon you that winning the competition was more than just an accidental achievement, as some may think, I shall have to relate to you something of my background and education. I won more than fifteen monetary awards and numerous honorable mentions—all in open competitions here and abroad. The reason that I inject personal references in my conversation is that the exacting details, specifications, and terms of contracts with statistics may be very dry to an outsider.

Just to set the record straight and to correct errors concerning the disputed Jefferson Nickel Competition, I wrote my life story for the reason that it might be of interest someday to a Jefferson nickel collector or numismatist.

My life story describes my studies at the former Royal Academy of Art in Munich, Germany, which I attended for seven years and which was at that time an exclusive school of classical tradition. Here I received an education in the practical arts as well as art history, architecture—and lectures and demonstrations in anatomy. Emphasis was placed on the spatial relationship of sculpture.

A chapter refers to my life as a front line soldier—my long hospitalization due to shrapnel wounds—my convalescence—my struggle to find my way back to normal life. During the last period of my convalescence I won first prize for my models for a monumental fountain and first prize for a Red Cross medal.

The revolution of 1918-1919 affected my life directly and seriously.

Another phase of my story touches on my experience as a mountain climber in the European Alps. Mountain climbing is exhilarating and challenging. It is beset with danger and adventure—like a call or defence to a personal contest. Climbing the peak of a mountain solo—you are very much alone, confronting an awesome spectacle such an enormity of dimensions, a closeness to the universe. There is an unearthly silence. You feel the tremendous power of all creation. After such revelation and drama you hesitate to return to daily city life—the contrast is so great, so startling. It influenced my mind and spirit—my attitude toward life, and prepared me well to endure all the hardships and struggles in later years, when at times everything around me seemed crashed.

Now my story comes to the 1930s. The life of most sculptors in the Depression years was rather hard, not at all lived in splendor. Sometimes I worked in ivory, other times I made window displays, other times I worked in silver, and for a half year I earned my living with a pick and a shovel, at the same time spending nights as a bus boy. Always on the move—New York, Chicago, Detroit, New York, and back to Chicago, where I finally could rent a studio, find artist friends, where I lived on big hopes, working long hours. Artists love good conversation, and our talks were interesting and lively.

The reward was that it lifted you spiritually, hardships were forgotten, and imagination raised beyond this world into one of eternal art—a dream. Sculptures

Felix Oscar Schlag, designer of the Jefferson nickel, receives a specimen from Eva Adams, director of the Mint. Jefferson nickels minted from 1938 through 1965 bore no indication of the designer. Beginning in 1966 the initials FS were added below the bust. This culminated a movement which began in the 1960s and which was encouraged by numismatists. A letter from Eva Adams dated February 9, 1966, to Senator Pat McNamara notes in part:

> "We are now striking five-cent pieces with the 1965 date, so it is too late to include the sculptor's initials on these coins. However, if later we find that the coin shortage situation has improved sufficiently to enable us to go to a later date on the nickels, this would be a logical time to engrave the sculptor's initials on master dies."

This was eventually done in 1966, and Schlag received a special Proof impression. (Coin World photo courtesy of Mrs. Marion Russell; letter quotation courtesy of Albert Bobrofsky)

were seen in a fabulous light—an inspiration to work—to fight with the material, that continued quest to find the concrete form, that elusive goal. The aim was always high and the works of the great artists of bygone days are where the shining star is. It is the mission of the artist to translate his time to which he is fixed, arrested, into a definite shape.

In the thirties the Section of Fine Arts, Washington, DC, sent leaflets to artists announcing competitions and news pertaining to government activities in relation to art. Late in 1937 or very early 1938, the department invited all American sculptors to compete for a new five-cent coin to be known as the Jefferson nickel. I believe it was the first and only open competition of this kind ever held in this country.

Prospective competitors were admonished that there were specific legal and other conditions which must be accurately complied with in creating a model, and that before proceeding, the competitors should get the specifications.

After receiving the detailed form announcement (regarding subject matter, size of models, coinage rules, etc.), I made a series of pencil sketches, without having an actual portrait in mind, just a composition—but the fundamental object for me was to find a likeness that portrayed the character and the strong facial features of the great American as I imagined him. None of the portraits of Jefferson in my collection satisfied me.

In my search I read everything I could find about Jefferson. I felt that unless I could somehow discover what I was looking for, my participation in the competition was uncertain. One night around 10 pm, after a hard day's work, I entered an old bookstore in my neighborhood to browse. To my great surprise and excitement, in the first magazine I opened I found a portrait of Jefferson that inspired me and which I intuitively knew depicted the nobel qualities of a true American statesman. The search was over—my decision to compete was certain!

In an open competition one has to strive harder than when the commission is given outright to a favored son. In open competition, the winning design is bound to be criticized more severely. Contemplate the disappointment of the other artists in the competition who also worked hard, spent many uncounted hours, and received no compensation whatsoever.

In submitting the design all the names of the participants were in individual sealed envelopes so that the jury would not be influenced by the name of someone known to them.

As I was occupied with other sculptural projects, the work on my interpretation, within the rules set up by the Treasury Department, forced me to work on the Jefferson nickel in the time spot from 10pm to 4am, at which time I retired for some rest.

To me as a sculptor, the Greek coins were always of the greatest interest. This is not to imply that other nations and cultures in different centuries did not create beautiful coins of the highest artistic value. I marveled at the freshness, technique, and beauty of Greek coins. There was an intensive drive and constant challenge to create the most beautiful designs, backed by a general understanding of art.

They represented a living force. Complete independence of Greek cities and communities was one reason for the variety of Greek coins. Even small cities had their own mints and jealously protected their rights and privileges.

The Greek coins are still exciting to me. Created in the negative, they give an effect one cannot imitate by modeling in clay or wax. And I applied the very same procedure, cutting the portrait as well as the reverse in plaster, always making tests.

The competition requirements were to submit the obverse and reverse sides of the coin. The subject matter on the obverse of the coin called for an authentic portrait of Jefferson. On the reverse side a representation of Monticello.

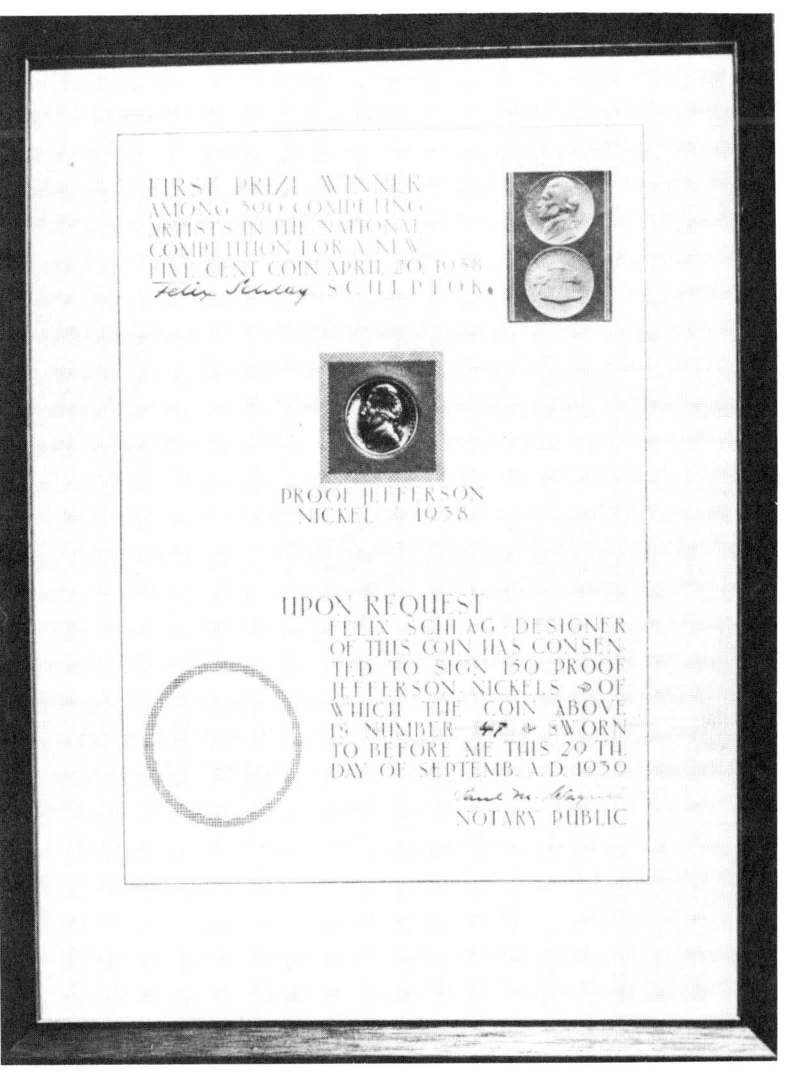

In 1939 Felix O. Schlag, designer of the Jefferson nickel, signed 150 framed displays featuring a Proof 1938 Jefferson nickel and photographs of the original design. The reverse of the original design portrayed Monticello from the corner view, unlike that eventually adopted for circulating coinage. (Coin World photograph)

The sculptor whose design won was required to execute a formal contract with the Treasury Department, agreeing among other things to make any revisions required by the Secretary of the Treasury without receiving any additional compensation.

Here are some quotes from the specifications.

"Neither the United States nor any officer of the government is liable to the sculptor for the use of any idea, plan, or design, express, executed, or submitted by the scuptor in connection with the work.

"The Treasury Department is under no obligation to show, exhibit, or preserve any work of the sculptors.

"If no designs are submitted which are of sufficient merit to justify an acceptance, no contract will be awarded as a result of this competition."

But even winning the competition—if the corrections asked were not made or accepted—you received no compensation at all.

It is interesting to note by comparison that the sculptor of the Peace silver dollar, who was given an outright commission by the government, received $2,500, and when the Treasury Department requested a minor change, the government paid all his expenses to come to Washington with his wife where they occupied the bridal suite at a first-class hotel with the government as host! This was back in 1921.

The models—in order to be acceptable—had to be of plaster not exceeding eight and one-half inches in diameter. The extreme depth of the relief was to be 5/32 of an inch. I finished all the models one day before the deadline, photographed them myself, and had to race to the proper train to get them off, for all the time spent would have been lost without even having a chance.

There were 390 pairs of models submitted by various artists. The reason for the large number of entries was the Depression, the prize money, and also the genuine desire to create a new coin, breaking the tradition of designs. The best sculptors in the country competed.

On April 20, 1938 I received a telegram from the superintendent of the Section of Painting and Sculpture asking for my biography. And the next day a telephone call gave me the good news that I had won the competition. But changes were requested. Nine suggestions were offered and I was advised to submit black and white drawings indicating the revisions. It meant starting all over again!

After submitting a new set of drawings, the director of the Mint advised me that they were very pleasing and that the fine qualities indicated in these drawings should be retained in the finished work and I should proceed with the modeling in clay and that photographs must be submitted before casting any plaster.

As I mentioned before—since my technique was to carve directly negative in plaster, I had no photos of any clay models to send for approval, but I submitted photos of the finished plaster models (which was a risk I took). Luckily enough they were accepted and I sent in the final models.

On July 21, 1938, Mrs. Nellie Tayloe Ross advised me that the acting secretary of the Treasury had approved the models and that Philadelphia was being instructed to surrender the prize money, $1,000. Considering the actual time involved to create the models, the reward in itself was nominal.

When the check arrived every cent was spent to pay debts accumulated due to sickness, death, and funeral expenses for someone close to me.

In that year, 1938, I finished a sculptural relief for the Whitehall, Illinois, post office. In 1939 I made twice life-size stone carvings for Chicago Heights, and also I created a smaller athletic group for Champaign, Illinois. In 1940 I worked on a relief of three runners.

The future seemed bright and promising.

Souvenir card sold for $2 in the 1960s by Felix O. Schlag, following his retirement in 1963. Albert Bobrofsky recalls that 400 such cards were produced, but it is possible that not all were sold.

Albert Bobrofsky (left) and Felix O. Schlag as photographed in 1965. Mr. Bobrofsky became a friend of the sculptor and had many discussions with him in the final years of Schlag's life. (Photographs on this page courtesy of Albert Bobrofsky)

There were inspiring offers for the Governor Horner Monument, one for Admiral Moffet, and an appointment with President Roosevelt was planned for the creation of a Marines Monument.

Then the war came. Planned commissions and promises of commissions were halted. Materials were difficult to obtain. All national, state, and personal interest in art was at a low. It seemed that everything that meant life to me was crashing. I spent time and money to get other commissions. My economic situation became desperate. I was over 50 years of age. I had no mechanical training—never worked in a factory. As a sculptor I had always maintained an optimistic and hopeful view. Even though I went through many adversities I kept my faith.

At the beginning of the war I tried to enlist in the United States Army. As I was still in good physical condition, I expected to be accepted. I had all my belongings packed and stored. Then came the letter from the War Department commending me for my patriotism, but refusing me because they said a man of my age could not stand the rigors of army life.

Since early youth photography was my hobby. I used it to photograph my own work. Now it appeared to be the only avenue of livelihood left to me. I opened my own portrait studio in Owosso, and luck was with me. One of the first photographs I took was of a young lady who was so pleased with it that she entered the portrait in a contest in California. It won her a first prize and a modeling career. This kind of news spread fast in a small city, and soon my appointment book was full.

After I had established a going business in photography, I had calls to do sculptural work, but by now I was accustomed to eating regularly and not having to wonder where my next meal was coming from or where I would obtain the next commission. It was the first time in my adult life that I felt a sense of security. I refused all offers of sculpture as none was a definite commission.

A few years ago I retired. The Jefferson nickel popped up again, and I was rediscovered due to the upsurge of interest in coin collecting. There were requests for my signature from collectors. One dealer came with a load of coin books to be signed. I found out that my signature was being sold, my letters of correspondence were used for personal advantage, books that I signed were being advertised for sale. At one coin show I saw mememto that I had given away priced at $500! I thought: I have the name so I might as well have the game. When I began asking $1.50 for a signature and $5.00 for an autographed card with a montage of the prize-winning designs of the nickel, the flood stopped. By this time you will have realized that the story of the Jefferson nickel is not an isolated event, but the story of a sculptor's trials and tribulations. It did not make me rich and famous.

Do not draw the conclusion that I have grown bitter toward life. Far from it—I still keep looking in the sky and at the stars and admire the often monumental beauty of creation.

THE 1939 DOUBLED DIE NICKEL

Bernard Nagengast, a well-known Ohio specialist in the Jefferson nickel series, furnished the author with information concerning the 1939 Doubled Die issue as well as other variations among early nickels in the series. A 1979 article featuring Mr. Nagengast noted that by that time he had examined more than 40,000 Uncirculated Jefferson nickels and along the way had discovered the first Mint State specimen of the 1943/2 overdate.

The first item is an article by Mr. Nagengast which appeared in "Coin World," February 28, 1979.

* * *

Jefferson Nickel Design Changes
By Bernard Nagengast

Little known to collectors is the fact that the Jefferson nickel has undergone numerous design changes through its history. Those changes have affected both obverse and reverse, and because the reverse changes are the most apparent, they will be discussed here.

The first such major change occurred in 1939, when the Mint strengthened the steps of Monticello. This was the only change that year, and it is interesting to note that the Jefferson nickel joins the Shield, Liberty and Buffalo Nickels, as well as several other series, with a change in the design during the first one or two years of coinage.

Why was the reverse modified? Malcolm Chell-Frost reported in the November 1942 *Numismatist* (page 797) as follows: "This is probably news to a great many collectors of nickels, but the truth is that the 1939, Jefferson nickel was reengraved in the early part of the year. Sometime before Feb. 21, 1939, the word MONTICELLO and the words FIVE CENTS were quite weak and the Mint decided to develop a new hub to strengthen these two or three words.

"Before this new hub was completed the old hub was cut over through MONTICELLO and FIVE CENTS. How many were made is strictly a guess; however, to give collectors an idea of how few are to be found they may be interested in a few figures.

"During the past two months I have had many collectors searching for this nickel," Chell-Frost wrote, "and up to the present 12 have been found. Here is a chance to do something during the day. I would greatly appreciate fellow collectors letting me know if any more are found and the amount.

"I quote a letter from the U.S. Mint written to me Sept. 18, 1939, as follows: 'Please be advised that a new hub was completed on the reverse Jefferson nickel with a slight increase in weight of MONTICELLO and FIVE CENTS, Feb. 21, 1939. Since that date all the dies have been drawn from the new hub. No change has been made in the hub since Feb. 21, 1939.' (Signed) Paul J. Dowd, acting superintendent. Thank you for replies."

If we take Dowd's letter at face value, it would appear that the master hub was changed, either the result of reduction from a new galvano, or by reengraving the hub itself. Dowd stated that the change was in "Monticello and five cents" and the context would appear to refer to the words MONTICELLO and FIVE CENTS.

A conflict arises, considering that these words show no change from the 1939 issues through the 1940 issues. The words appear identical in strength on both reverses used in 1939. Was Dowd in error?

I propose that his letter referred to the reverse change which did occur, but considering that his letter was written many months after the modification, his

1939 DOUBLED DIE NICKEL

One of the most interesting mint errors of modern times is the 1939 Jefferson nickel with MONTICELLO and FIVE CENTS doubled on the reverse. This variety was not widely recognized by numismatists until most coins had achieved a generous degree of circulation, with the result that specimens seen today are apt to show extensive wear. (Photograph courtesy of Bernard Nagengast)

memory of the change was a bit confused, and he was in error stating that the change was in Monticello and five cents.

He should have stated that the change was in Monticello, referring to the step change.

The next mystery, Chell-Frost's referral to a "cut over" 1939 issue in the words MONTICELLO and FIVE CENTS is not such a problem when you consider that there is a doubled die reverse existing in 1939. I believe Chell-Frost discovered some of the doubled die reverses in 1942, remembered his correspondence with the Mint in 1939, and took Dowd's referral to "Monticello and Five Cents" to literally refer to MONTICELLO and FIVE CENTS.

Since the Variety I doubled die reverse, pictured in the *Guidebook of U.S. Coins*, has the most visible doubling on these words, it would seem entirely logical to Chell-Frost that the doubling was reengraving, and the Mint had reengraved the letters just prior to preparing the new hub which supposedly had stronger lettering.

One fact makes his reasoning wrong—the major 1939 doubled die reverse is a double hub (Class III—design hub doubling), not a reengraving, and it is of the second reverse design, the one with the strengthened steps. This would mean the doubled die was produced after the hub modification early in 1939.

To summarize this rather confusing story, the reverse of the Jefferson nickel was modified in early 1939 to strengthen the details of the steps of Monticello, apparently due to Mint dissatisfaction with the poor detail of the original design. This was the only change in the reverse design I can find for that year.

The new reverse was used for the remainder of 1939, through the year 1970, with no further modification. A major doubled die reverse was produced in 1939, using the second type reverse, apparently by improper registering of the die blank to the hub between hubbings (the die blank must be hubbed, then taken off the hubbing press and annealed to soften it, then hubbed again to get all the hub detail into the die). There was apparently only one working die made with the major doubling, although other dies are known with less noticeable doubling.

What designation should numismatists give to this design change? Normally, the first or second year design changes have been called "Type One and Type Two". We already have that description being used with Jefferson nickels, referring to the wartime alloy change in 1942 on the Philadelphia Mint issue.

The only logical alternative to avoid confusion would be to call the first type reverse of 1939, the "reverse of 38", since that reverse was used on all issues of 1939. The second reverse could then be called "reverse of 40", since that reverse appears on all 1940 issues.

By now, many of you are probably itching to know how many were made of each reverse type. The Mint figures for P, D and S 1939 issues are not broken down into the two types, but general conclusions can be drawn. During the past two years I have looked at more than 1,000 1939 Uncirculated coins of all three Mints, and found that (1) The 1939 reverse of 1938 does not seem to exist in great quantity, with no solid rolls found. (2) The 1939 reverse of 1940 is far more common for Philadelphia, with most rolls checked being solid rolls of this type, and a minority of the rolls having up to 10 pieces of the reverse of 1938 mixed in. (3) The 1939-D seems to be almost evenly divided between the two reverses. (4) The 1939-S is more common with the reverse of 1938, with most rolls being solid reverse of 1938 rolls and most of the remainder mixed.

The fact that the 1939 Philadelphia issue is much more common with the reverse of 1940, lends credence to believing the master hub was modified in early 1939. In order to get working dies to the branch Mints for the 1939 coinage, the Mint would have had to begin work late in 1938, when the old hub was being used. By the time the hub was modified, many dies would have already been sent to the branch Mints. The Philadelphia personnel may have also elected to use most of the new design dies themselves to allow quick reaction to any production problems that might arise with the new reverse.

Since the Denver and San Francisco Mints produced few coins in 1939, they didn't have much chance to produce large quantities with the new reverse. Thus by percentage, the Philadelphia coinage with the reverse of 1938 was apparently quite small, perhaps one-fifth of the 1939 issue.

This is not to say that the Denver and San Francisco issues are common in any type reverse. Due to the small mintage, all 1939-D and 1939-S Uncirculated coins, regardless of reverse type, are scarce, with the 1939-S appearing to be scarcer than the higher priced 1939-D. The previous discussion refers to the circulation strikes only.

1938 Proof nickels employ the reverse of 1938, as do most 1939 Proof nickels. However, as of summer 1984 I know of fewer than 50 each of Proof 1939 nickels with the reverse of 1940 and 1940 nickels with the reverse of 1938.

* * *

In August 1984 Bernard Nagengast wrote to the author with additional information on the 1939 Doubled Die Jefferson nickel, here quoted in part:

"This variety was discovered in the early 1940s in New York City by subway token collectors, and a copy of a letter from one of them [L. Friedman] is enclosed. Incidentally, I had an opportunity to purchase a number of circulated Doubled Die reverse (Variety 1) pieces from a retired New York subway man recently. He said, 'Everybody was looking for them at the time—this must have been like the 1955 Doubled Die cent craze!

"Because the variety was discovered a few years after issue, Uncirculated specimens are quite rare. I have seen personally, or know of about 12 pieces in various Uncirculated gradations, four of which were found by a collector in an Uncirculated roll of 1939 nickels which he examined in 1980. I would estimate that fewer than 50 Uncirculated coins exist."

* *

The following letter, from Louis Friedman, was sent to "Coin World" after Mr. Nagengast wrote on the subject of 1939 Doubled Die pieces. Excerpts from Mr. Friedman's letter of July 23, 1979 are reprinted herewith:

"First, may I introduce myself as being one of the New York City transit clerks referred to in the article, having worked there from 1937 through 1946, and may I say that in those years about 25% of the advertisers in 'The Numismatist' and the 'Numismatic Scrapbook Magazine'—the only two numismatic publications at the time—were co-workers of mine on the New York City transit system. From that list of 35 or 40 people, there are only three active dealers at the present time: Herbert Tobias of New York City, Max L. Kaplan of Florida, and myself...

"Over a period of years I have been able to find about 500 pieces in Very Good to AU grades and sold most of them long ago for about $15 per roll.

"I will just touch on the 1942/1 dime. There was an article in 'The Numismatist' shortly after these were released. I cannot recall the author, who found one in the area near Kingston, New York. After reading the article, the next day I searched for them and found one. I showed it to Joe Stack, who was then on 46th Street in New York City, and we agreed on a price of $5. I immediately let my co-workers know that I was buying them at $2.50, and at the end of the day I had picked up 10 pieces, which he bought. They started to come in faster, and Mr. Chell-Frost took several hundred from me, the late Maurice Gould bought several hundred from me also, and I was shipping them as fast as I got them to buyers all over the country. Then my competitors got them, and the prices started to drop. You will find these listings in my advertisements of 1943, 1944, 1945, etc.

"It gave me a great thrill a few years ago to attend a meeting of the Los Angeles Coin Club and see a slide program by Karl Brainard, founder of the Numismatic Association of Southern California. He showed a photograph of the 1942/1 dime which he purchased from me when I still lived in Brooklyn. I also have a letter from Mr. Sydney P. Noe, secretary of the American Numismatic Society, dated January 10, 1944, expressing their appreciation for a 1942/1 dime. Mr. Kortjohn presented it to them on my behalf.

"I am glad I had the pleasure of exploiting this coin and still get favorable comments from former customers."—Louis Friedman

Collecting Half Dimes

1792-1873

The 1792 Half Disme

Half dimes or silver five-cent pieces were *regularly* coined from 1794 through 1873. Prefacing the series is one of the most interesting and romantic of all American coins: the 1792 half disme spelled with an "s" in the middle of the word.

In 1792 President George Washington in his annual address specifically mentioned the 1792 half disme as being the first product of the newly established Philadelphia Mint. Legend has it that the silver to coin the approximately 1,500 pieces was personally provided by President Washington in order to expedite production of the coins.

The design of the 1792 half disme closely follows the famous Birch pattern cents of the same year. The obverse features a head of Miss Liberty, modeled, as some suggest, after Martha Washington (but the attribution is doubtful), surrounded by the inscription LIB. PAR. OF SCIENCE & INDUSTRY. The reverse shows a bird (an eagle?) in flight, with inscription surrounding.

Although officially intended as a pattern issue, 1792 half dismes were placed into circulation as a means of exchange. This was done at the time of issue, with George Washington noting that they were struck to fill a demand for them in the channels of commerce. So, it is appropriate to list the 1792 half disme as the first circulating coin in the half dime series. Whether it is a *regular* issue or whether it should simply be construed as a *pattern* is a subject of debate. From a strictly legal viewpoint it is a pattern. However, as nearly all of the mintage was actually used in circulation, a case can be made that it should be included as part of the general half dime series. Either way, the piece is mentioned here because of its interesting nature. However, it is appropriate to note that the majority of half dime collectors as well as those forming type sets have *not* included this particular piece as part of the regular series.

Approximately 100 to 200 specimens of this coin survive today. Nearly all of them show extensive wear, with Good to Fine being representative grades. Many years ago I acquired a full Uncirculated coin from Cincinnati dealer Sol Kaplan, but apart from that purchase I have seen no equivalent piece.

1794-1795 Flowing Hair Half Dimes

The first large quantity production of half dimes (the "s" from disme by this time had been dropped) occurred in 1794. The obverse of the 1794-1795 style, known as the Flowing Hair type, features Miss Liberty facing to the right, with stars to the left and right borders, LIBERTY above, and the date below. The Small Eagle reverse illustrates a delicate bird perched at the center of a wreath, with the inscription UNITED STATES OF AMERICA surrounding. The piece bears no indication of denomination. Indeed, it was not until 1829 that half dimes indicated that they were worth five cents. Citizens were supposed to know the value by the size and weight. At the time the acceptance of a coin in commerce at a given value was predicated upon the metal in which the coin was struck and its apparent weight and diameter. Coins in circulation consisted of a confused jumble of foreign issues of varying sizes, weights, states of wear, and regularity. Valuations tended to be approximate.

Half dimes of 1795 are of the same design used in 1794. Many die varieties exist of these early issues, all of which are attributed in *The United States Half Dimes*, by D.W. Valentine, published by the American Numismatic Society in 1931. This followed the pioneering effort, *The Early Half Dimes of the United States*, published by Harold P. Newlin in 1883. Newlin, an attorney, enjoyed his coins (which comprised many other series in addition to half dimes) immensely, and part of his affection is evident when reading his book. Coins of the year 1802 in particular were fascinating to him. In 1984 Jules Reiver published a reference and identification system for half dimes based on the Valentine book.

It is unfortunate that more numismatic references are not written with a spirit of love and enjoyment. Among references of our own era, Dr. Sheldon's *Penny Whimsy* has ample charisma, but too many others are simply dry and dull recitations or listings. Anecdotes, experiences, and a certain amount of spice are not only interesting, but reflect the spirit of the true collector.

HALF DIMES 1794-1795

Shown on this page are several different specimens of 1794 and 1795 half dimes. The Flowing Hair obverse with the Small Eagle motif was produced only in these two years. There are many die varieties. Note, for example, the differences between the two 1794 half dimes to the left. At casual glance they appear identical, but upon close inspection such features as the relationship of the first and last digits of the date to the hair and neck, the number of leaves at the apex of the wreath reverse and their relationship to the letters, and other features are distinctively different.

The three 1795 half dimes are likewise different. The first exhibits a prominent diebreak at the upper right of the obverse, above TY and the adjacent star. The border below the date has the denticles (minute serrations) weakly defined. On the reverse, mint-caused file marks or adjustment marks are visible at the bottom border below the eagle. The second 1795 half dime, while quite sharp on the obverse, shows weakness at striking at the center of the reverse. The third piece shows prominent adjustment marks on the obverse, brushing the cheek of Miss Liberty and extending into the hair.

Whereas years ago numismatists collected half dimes by Valentine varieties, in recent decades few have been able to afford such activity. Most sets of half dimes from 1794 through the end of the series in 1873 are comprised of major date and mintmark varieties or, in the instance of type sets, one each of the major designs.

It is appropriate to mention adjustment marks, a situation common to other early silver (and gold) issues as well. Silver, a precious metal, was included in early United States coins to full intrinsic value. The half dimes of 1794 and 1795 (for example) contained approximately five cents worth of silver at the time of issue. During this period the United States monetary system was relatively new and untried, and the public was skeptical of it (is the public more confident now?). As a result, the intrinsic value concept was important to the public. Coins were given full metallic weight.

When planchets were prepared for early half dimes (bear in mind that these remarks apply to other early silver and gold coins as well) each piece was weighed to make certain it was accurate. If a piece was significantly underweight the planchet was melted. If the piece was overweight it was scraped with a file to remove the excess metal. At one time an entire room at the Philadelphia Mint was occupied by women sitting in front of balance scales with files in hand! These file marks are still visible on many if not most half dimes of 1794-1795. These marks show up in the form of parallel striations usually visible on the obverse and reverse at the highest spots—in the hair of Miss Liberty or on the breast or wings of the eagle, or sometimes toward the rim or border. These adjustment marks are normal and are to be expected. Most advanced collectors are familiar with them, but often a beginning collector will confuse adjustment marks with scratches. Scratches, of course, are marks put on a coin after striking. Whereas scratches would seriously affect a coin's value, adjustment marks do not unless they are especially severe.

As the Mint-caused adjustment marks were made by file marks in the planchet before the coin was struck, after striking, the adjustment marks remain parallel to each other and also follow the "hills and dales" of the surface characteristics. That is, an adjustment mark might begin at the rim, continue through the border of the rim to the field, through the edge of a star, across a star, out the other side of the star, back into the field again, and so on. On the other hand, a scratch produced later would tend to be deepest on the highest parts of the coin and perhaps not visible at all in the lower areas, for the lower areas were protected by the features in relief. Further, whereas file marks or adjustment marks made on the planchet caused a *removal* of metal, scratches made later caused a *displacement* of metal, so under microscopic examination a scratch will usually show a ridge of metal on one or both sides (unless it has been worn away). Perhaps the present discussion is a bit complicated. To paraphrase the old proverb, examining one coin is worth a thousand words of description.

Although 1794 half dimes were a novelty when they were released, apparently the citizenry felt generally indifferent about them, for few if any were saved as curiosities. Issues of both 1794 and 1795 are exceedingly rare in Uncirculated grade, with 1794 being considerably the rarer of the two. Although exact mintage breakdowns are not known for the years (86,416 pieces were made for the combined period), the survival of pieces today indicates that perhaps three or four times as many 1795 half dimes were made than of those dated 1794. The typical specimen encountered today is apt to be in worn condition.

Precisely who engraved dies for various coins during the formative years of the Philadelphia Mint is not known. Research by Robert W. Julian, Walter H. Breen, Don Taxay, and other scholars has resulted in certain postulations, one of which is that Robert Scot, employed at the Mint as an engraver at the time, was the designer of the 1794-1795 half dime and certain other denominations of these years.

1796-1797 Half Dimes

In 1796 the half dime design was changed to the Draped Bust obverse with Small Eagle reverse. Although the eagle is small on this as well as the 1794-1795 type, it is differently styled on the later issues. On half dimes of 1796-1797 the eagle appears more substantial; less delicate.

The obverse portrays Miss Liberty with a draped bosom facing right, with stars and inscription somewhat similar to the earlier issues. It was at first proposed that 13 stars be used as a standard for American coinage, but as additional states joined the Union, more stars were added. Thus in 1797, half dimes with 15 stars on the obverse and, finally, 16 stars were created. At that point it was realized that the star increments had seemingly unlimited potential, and soon there would be no room left on the front of the coin for anything else! So, the 13-star format was reverted to in later years.

The first issue among 1796-1797 half dimes is an overdate, 1796/5. This indicates that a Draped Bust coinage of 1795 was contemplated, but such coinage never materialized, and "1795 Draped Bust" half dimes exist only in overdate form.

Another variety of the 1796 half dime is the so-called LIKERTY issue. This is really not deserving of being called a separate variety, although tradition has dictated listing it as such in reference books. What appears to be an erroneous K is not a K at all but is simply a B which was originally perfect in the die but, which over a period of time, became worn at the top so that part is no longer visible. Don Taxay, in his *Comprehensive Encyclopedia of United States Coins* (published in 1971 and 1976), stated the situation perfectly when he noted that the coin is collected "due to the mistaken notion that it is a blundered die."

The 1797 half dimes comprise three different varieties—with 13, 15, and 16 stars on the obverse. These intentional star varieties are in contrast with engraving errors, daydreaming, or whatever caused such unexplained anomalies as the 1817 large cent with 15 stars, the 1828 half cent with 12 stars, and the 1832 $5 with 12 stars.

HALF DIMES
1796-1797

Half dimes of the 1796 and 1797 years are of the Draped Bust obverse type in combination with the Small Eagle reverse design. The "small eagle" is different from that of the 1794 and 1795 years. While the 1796 is sharply struck, the 1797 shown to the left is weakly impressed. The eagle on the reverse appears as an outline, without feather details. This is characteristic of genuine specimens of the issue. Of all American silver design types, the half dimes of 1796 and 1797 are among the most elusive.

To the right is shown an interesting variety of 1800, the so-called "LIBEKTY" issue. This is a result not of a die error but of an imperfect punch. The R appears as a K. The variety is not particularly scarce.

1800-1805

Half dimes of the 1800 through 1805 years (minted continuously with the exception of 1804) bear the Draped Bust obverse design in combination with the heraldic eagle reverse. With relatively few exceptions, examples seen today, particularly in the later dates in the range, are weakly struck. The 1805 half dime shown at the bottom of the page illustrates this characteristic.

In this date range is to be found the 1802 half dime, one of the foremost American silver rarities.

High-grade half dimes of the 1796-1797 type are extremely rare. When collecting photographs for his *Photograde* grading book, James F. Ruddy found that well preserved examples of this issue were harder to find than were any other major United States coin types, including designs that were much higher priced. It is very often the case that catalogue values have little to do with rarity or, for that matter, the frequency of appearance of pieces on the market. In the 1970s, when David Akers published a series of six volumes covering the frequency of auction appearances of various gold coins from dollars through double eagles, his findings upset a number of traditions. Certain coins long considered to be rarities seemed to be plentiful, and numerous "common" pieces were so elusive that examples in certain grades had not crossed the auction block in years! This sort of circumstance contributes to the thrill of the chase. If everything about United States coins were known to the last decimal point there would be nothing left for the imagination, no new discoveries, no room for individuality, no opportunity for research, no chance to acquire sleepers or bargains. As it is, the numismatist who takes time to study coins can find many unappreciated items available for reasonable prices, just financial reward for the efforts expended in seeking them out.

In worn grades half dimes of the 1796-1797 years are scarce. Although as of this writing the 13, 15, and 16-star varieties of 1797 bear virtually identical listings in the *Guide Book*, availability is not the same for all issues. Someone like David Akers probably is needed to patiently digest old auction records and sale appearances to tell us the true story.

The 1796/5 overdate is a rarity in all conditions. It, too, does not list for significantly more than others of its design. In Uncirculated condition the issue most often seen is the normal (not overdate) 1796. This seems to be several times more plentiful than 1797. In addition to displaying adjustment marks, which are often seen, half dimes of 1797 tend to be weakly defined on the reverse, with the eagle sometimes appearing simply as an outline, without detailed feathers. Like half cents, large cents, and other issues of this era, these early half dimes have *personalities*. Not only is each die variety different, each coin encountered seems to be different from the one before or after it. Such adds the undefinable quality which Dr. Sheldon characterized as *charm*.

1800-1805 Heraldic Eagle Half Dimes

No half dimes were minted with the dates 1798 or 1799. A new design appeared in 1800. The obverse motif was the Draped Bust style as used earlier, but the reverse now displayed a Heraldic Eagle, somewhat resembling the Great Seal of the United States. Shown is a wing-spread eagle with stars and clouds above. The Heraldic Eagle is rather "traditional," and has appeared from time to time on our coinage. Used on silver and gold issues until 1807, the general style then gave way to other designs. Then in 1892, when Barber quarters and half dollars made their appearance, the Heraldic Eagle reverse was revived. In 1916, when new designs for the quarter and half dollar appeared, the Heraldic Eagle reverse was abandoned. Anyone believing that it would never be used again was incorrect, for when the Kennedy half dollar appeared in 1964 the Heraldic Eagle reverse was used, though with a modernistic treatment.

The subject of art in coin design is one that has been debated for centuries. Is the function of a coin to serve only as a medium of commerce, or should it have artistic values as well? When one reviews coinage of the present era, such pieces often seem quite bland in comparison to earlier pieces. But, one has only to read the *American Journal of Numismatics* or other publications of a century ago to learn that back then current designs were not liked either! A superb, but generally overlooked book, *Numismatic Art in America*, by Cornelius Vermeule, is subtitled *Aesthetics of the United States Coinage.* While this volume has not been in the mainstream of numismatics (perhaps because it lists neither values nor investment recommendations), it is deserving of great recognition. The dust jacket tells it all:

> "Coins are a form of art to which every American is exposed—the only class of sculpture with which many will ever come in contact. Yet coins have been the least respected and understood of art forms in the United States. In spite of the awakening of interest in the American series and the ever-increasing numbers of devoted enthusiasts and numismatists, the public remains largely ignorant of the aesthetics of the coin or medal. Catalogues and technical descriptions proliferate, United States coins are subjected to intensive study as collectors' items, yet even among art historians and students of American culture this rich field of iconography and medallic art has been neglected."

The new half dime design with Heraldic Eagle reverse was continued through 1805, after which the denomination was suspended until 1829, when the Capped Bust style made its debut.

The rather brief 1800-1805 Draped Bust obverse, Heraldic Eagle reverse style has few major varieties. One variation noted is the so-called 1800 LIBEKTY piece. This is not a blundered die or even a true variety, but is simply the result of a defective "R" punch having been used. This is somewhat analogous to the situation dealing with the 1796 "LIKERTY" coin—also a non-variety.

This era contains one of the most prominent of all American rarities—the 1802 half dime. In years past the appearance of one of these in an auction sale or other offering would create quite a bit of attention. In recent times the piece has been relegated to simply a catalogue listing, noticeable only by the value of the 1802 being significantly higher than of the half dimes before or after. Our numismatic predecessors decades ago appreciated the 1802 half dime as a "sentimental rarity" and provided quite a bit of space whenever one came up for sale.

I happen to like the 1802 half dime, and whenever one appears in an Auctions by Bowers and Merena sale I enjoy handling it. Perhaps some of this liking is traced to Harold Newlin's thoughts printed in his 1883 monograph on the series. In Newlin's words:

> "I think it may be interesting to collectors to learn about this—the most desirable piece of the American silver series. I foresee that some numismatists will take issue with me in this statement—that the 1802 half dime is the most desirable of the silver series.
>
> "My reason for giving it the most exalted place, I will endeavor to explain. If a collector were asked to name the other four rarest American silver coins he would, I am sure, naming them in order of their denominations, say: 1804 silver dollar, 1823 quarter, 1827 quarter and 1802 half dime. I assume that these are the rarest.
>
> "The 1804 dollar has been restruck. The dies were not destroyed until the year 1869, and I believe that pieces were restruck from the dies upon two occasions a short time prior to this year.
>
> "Disgraceful as this fact is, it is true that these pieces were restruck in the United States Mint by some of its employees, no doubt for speculation; and a restruck specimen now graces the Mint Cabinet and is described in the most glowing terms to strangers, as one of the most valuable pieces in the collection worth, no doubt, $1,000.
>
> "The custodians of the collection know full well that their piece is a restrike for I am indebted to one of them for this information. I wonder why they allow the piece to remain, testifying as it does to the past queer doings of the Mint.
>
> "The 1827 quarter has also been restruck. The 1823 quarter is struck from the altered die of the quarter of the preceding year and possesses no characteristics of its own. The 1802 half dime is open to none of these objections. It has never been restruck. The dies were made for that year and destroyed. I have seen many dangerous counterfeits of the 1804 dollar and the 1823 quarter, but I have never seen one of the 1802 half dime.
>
> "Upon these facts I base my opinion that the half dime of 1802 is the most desirable of the silver series."

Newlin's logic is not exactly faultless (would all 1802 half dimes become undesirable should a counterfeit example of one of these appear on the market?), but one cannot criticize his enthusiasm for the subject—and enthusiasm is certainly part of collecting coins.

A strange thing about the 1802 half dime is the virtually complete absence of specimens in higher grades. A Very Fine coin would be unusual, an Extremely Fine piece would be a landmark, and a full Uncirculated example is not known.

Probably two dozen or so 1802 half dimes are known today. Most of these are in grades from About Good to Fine. Often a span of a year or two or three will elapse between appearances at auctions.

In general, half dimes of the 1800-1805 type (it should be noted that no examples were made with the date 1804) are seen only in lower grades. A few Uncirculated 1800 half dimes have come on the market from time to time, but examples of any other date of this design are extreme rarities. Difficulties with striking—the metal flow problem—occur with the majority of half dimes of this type, with the result that the stars to the upper right of the eagle's head on the reverse are lightly impressed or invisible. At the time the Mint was not turning out coins for collectors to view under magnification. Indeed, as far as is known not a single person in America collected United States coins by dates at the time. Rather, production was strictly utilitarian—to issue as many pieces in the least amount of time with the least amount of effort.

1829-1837 Capped Bust Half Dimes

In 1829 a new half dime design made its appearance, the Capped Bust type, a style following that used on half dollars from 1807 through 1836. No half dimes were minted of the years 1806 through 1828 inclusive. Had they been, the Capped Bust design would have been introduced earlier, as it was with other denominations.

This style of half dime was minted with little variation from 1829 through 1837 inclusive. Some differences occur in lettering sizes, but most numismatists seek examples only by dates or, in the instance of type collectors, a single specimen of the design. One interesting variety of 1834 has the 3 in the date punched backwards and then corrected! This is a rather spectacular blunder when viewed with a low-powered magnifying glass. While "tradition" has been responsible for the listing in coin references and the popularization of the 1796 LIKERTY and the 1800 LIBEKTY non-varieties, the 1834 with backwards 3 in the date has been overlooked by virtually everyone! Unlike love and war, apparently all is not fair in numismatics!

Half dimes of this type are readily available in a wide variety of grades from very worn through Uncirculated. Around 1970 my firm purchased a small hoard of 50 Choice Uncirculated 1835 half dimes from William K. Raymond. Offered at a price that seems an unbelievable bargain a decade later, the pieces found ready buyers. In proportion to the demand for them, Choice Uncirculated specimens of the various dates of the 1829-1837 design seem to be elusive. Issues of the year 1837 are particularly hard to find in this preservation.

Many years ago I was intrigued, and thought it ironic, when a local woman telephoned to say that she had an 1835 half dime. She brought it to the office, and it indeed proved to be half of a dime—an 1835 dime had been cut in two pieces with a tinsnips years ago! The owner did not realize that on its own the term *half dime* had another meaning. I carried this piece around in my wallet for a number of years and then misplaced it. It was always a fun item to show to another dealer! Then I read an account of the monetary situation in the Louisiana-Texas area during the 1830s and 1840s and was surprised to learn that from time to time United States coins such as dimes and quarters were snipped into fractional pieces to make small change. So, the 1835 "half dime" might have had special numismatic importance after all.

1837-1873 Liberty Seated Half Dimes

Half dimes of the 1837-1873 Liberty Seated style are divided into several sub-types, as the following descriptions indicate. The design commenced in 1837 when a new obverse motif, the product of engraver Christian Gobrecht, made its appearance. This design, featuring Miss Liberty seated on a rock and holding a shield, was first envisioned in 1835 and was first used on the pattern silver dollars of 1836. However, the debut of the style on coins made for circulation occurred with the half dime and dime of 1837.

The first Liberty Seated style, without stars on obverse, was struck at the Philadelphia Mint in 1837 and at the New Orleans Mint in 1838. The absence of stars gives the coin a particularly appealing cameo-like appearance which many numismatists feel is more attractive than the later with-stars modification. It is a shame that this piece was not continued for a longer time.

The *Guide Book* lists mintage figures as 1,405,000 for the 1837 Philadelphia issue and just 70,000 for 1838-O. Fortunately for numismatists, quite a few 1837 Philadelphia coins were saved at or around the time of issue, with the result that Uncirculated pieces are seen with some frequency today. Years ago our firm handled these in pairs, trios, and other small groups, but today the supply has become so widely dispersed that even a single piece offered in an auction catalogue usually merits a picture and a detailed enthusiastic description. Circulated examples of 1837 are much more plentiful and can be obtained without difficulty. The price has risen in recent years due to the demand as a design type.

On the other hand, 1838-O is scarce. While worn specimens, up to and including Extremely Fine and AU, can be obtained with only a modest amount of searching, Choice Uncirculated coins are great rarities. The number of specimens that are *truly* in this condition can probably be counted on the fingers of one hand with, as they say, some fingers left over. The same situation is true of the 1838-O dime without obverse stars.

Cover of Scott's 1887 catalogue. This paperbound pamphlet achieved wide circulation among numismatists and was one of the first comprehensive guides available to collectors.

	Uncirculated	Fine	Good
1802		100 00	30 00
1803	10 00	4 00	2 00
1805	15 00	6 00	3 00
1829 Head to left	40	15	10
1830	40	20	10
1831	40	20	10
1832	30	15	10
1833	40	20	10
1834	40	20	10
1835 large date	40	15	10
1835 small date	50	25	15
1836	50	20	10
1837 Head to left	50	20	10
1837 Liberty seated	25	15	10
1838 no stars	3 00	1 00	30
1838 with "	25	15	10
1839	30	15	10
1840 no drapery	2 00	30	20
1840 with "	40	15	10
1841	40	15	10
1842	40	15	10
1843	40	15	10
1844	50	20	10
1845	25	15	10
1846	15 00	4 00	2 00
1847	25	15	10
1848 small date	25	15	10
1848 large date	50	25	15
1849	25	15	10
1850	25	15	10
1851	25	15	10
1852	40	25	10
1853 no arrows at date	40	25	10

	Proof	Uncirc.	Fine	Good
1853 with arrows	40	20	15	10
1854	40	20	15	10
1855	40	20	15	10
1856 no arrows	40	20	15	10
1857	40	20	15	10
1858	40	20	15	10
1859	40	20	15	10
1860 with stars	4 00	3 00	2 00	1 50
1860 without stars	40	20	15	10
1861	40	20	15	10
1862	40	20	15	10
1863	1 00	50	30	20
1864	1 50	1 00	50	30
1865	1 00	50	30	20
1866	1 00	50	30	20
1867	1 00	50	30	20
1868	1 00	50	30	20
1869	1 00	50	30	20
1870	50	25	15	10
1871	50	20	15	10
1872	50	20	15	10
1873	1 00	40	30	10

Silver Three Cent Pieces.

	Proof	Uncirc.	Fine	Good
1851 Star in centre	50	25	15	10
1851 New Orleans mint	1 00	50	25	15
1852	50	25	15	10
1853	50	25	15	10
1854	1 00	30	20	15
1855	4 00	2 00	50	20
1856	1 00	30	15	10
1857	1 00	50	25	10
1858	50	25	10	8
1859	40	15	10	8
1860	50	25	15	10
1861	40	15	10	8
1862	40	15	10	8
1863	2 00	1 50	1 00	50
1864	2 00	1 50	1 00	50
1865	1 50	1 25	75	50
1866	1 50	1 00	60	40
1867	1 50	1 00	60	40
1868	2 00	1 50	1 00	50
1869	2 00	1 50	1 00	50
1870	1 00	50	40	20
1871	1 00	75	50	25
1872	1 00	75	50	25
1873	1 50	1 40	1 30	1 25

Bronze War Medals.

Prussian, Alsen, 1864	1 00
Francis Joseph of Austria	1 00
Doppel Cross, 1864	1 50
Prussia, 1815, For faithful duty	1 50
Papal States against V. Immanuel, silvered	3 00
Francis Joseph, 1873	1 00
Egypt. 1882, 5-pointed star, Nile	4 00
Maximilian, for military merit	5 00
G. A. R. badges, 5-pointed star, various ranks	1 50
City of Brooklyn Veterans Medal 1866	5 00
Roumanian, iron cross	1 50
Hanover, George V, brass gilt	1 50
Louis XVIII, silver gilt and enamel	2 00
" same, larger	5 00
New ribbons for medals in large variety, each	50

This page from "Scott's Standard Catalogue of Gold & Silver Coins," 1887 edition, shows half dimes (left column) and silver three-cent pieces. Wouldn't it be nice to be able to buy Proof half dimes dated in the 1850s for 40 cents each today!!!

COIN CABINETS.

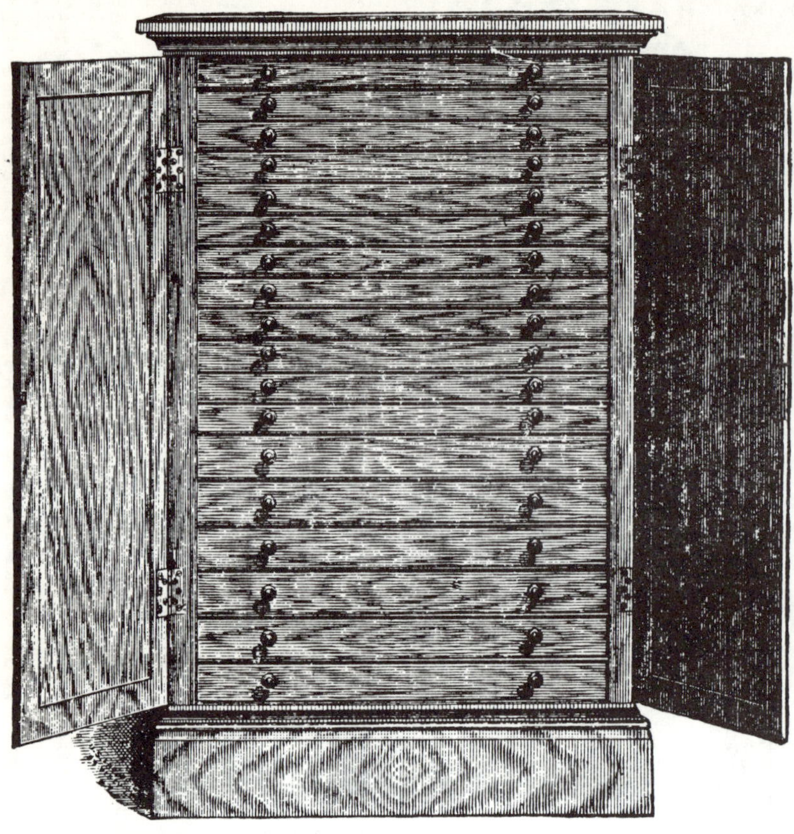

THE SCOTT STAMP & COIN CO, L'D are pleased to announce to Collectors that they are manufacturing COIN CABINETS of the following sizes and styles:

No. 1 size, 24½ x 17½, eighteen drawers each 15 x 9 inches, and from 3-8 to 6-8 inches deep, two doors with lock and key, polished black walnut; very handsome and durable. Price $10.00. Boxing 50c., extra.

No. 2, size 14¾ x 15½, twelve drawers each 13 x 7; 5-16 in. deep, door with lock and key, polished black walnut, very handsome and durable. Price $6.00. Boxing, &c., 50c. extra.

These are made by first-class workmen, with the aid of fine machinery, thus producing a cabinet which is both strong and elegant, the price being at least 50 per cent less than the cost of the same piece of furniture when made for private parties. Any desired style made to order, the price being about a half more for the same amount of work when made singly.

In the 1880s it was fashionable to keep coin collections in cabinets. The style shown here is representative of the era.

Permit me to digress on the subject of rarity and the quantity of a particular coin known to exist. The number of examples that can be traced of a given issue is useful information for the numismatist. For some issues, a low mintage indicates that few pieces are known. In general, for a given issue the number of *worn* pieces is roughly proportional to the number originally struck. That is, if one million pieces were struck of issue A, and one hundred thousand pieces were struck of issue B, then issue B today is ten times rarer than issue A. This applies only to pieces that have seen circulation. Uncirculated coins are another thing entirely. Proofs add another dimension or complication, for Proof mintages usually have little to do with business strike mintages.

Focusing on Proofs, I point out coins of the decade of the 1880s of which Proof nickel three-cent pieces, quarter dollars, half dollars, and $3 gold pieces generally are much more often seen than are Uncirculated business strikes, although both categories are elusive. Were it not for the fact that ample Proofs were made of these issues, examples of these dates would be exceedingly rare today.

The number of surviving Proofs can be estimated by reading the mintage figures. As Proofs of a given issue, with relatively few exceptions, went to numismatists who paid premiums for them, most were saved and given a degree of care. To be sure, some were "spent," others received hairlines or scratches, and still others drifted to other fates. But, by and large, a reasonable proportion of the original Proof mintage still survives today. Of a given silver issue of the 1860s, for example, probably 50% to 75% of the Proofs can be traced, although the majority are apt to have some defects.

Uncirculated coins are much more difficult to evaluate in terms of survival. David Akers, in his gold coin studies mentioned earlier, surveyed auction appearances of various denominations from the gold dollar through the double eagle and concluded that certain pieces appeared less frequently than the mintages or tradition would indicate, and others were more common than believed. The student endeavoring to do research using auction catalogues more than a few years old will run into a grading problem. It was the custom in years past to grade coins very loosely. Time after time, when cataloguing for sale today coins housed in envelopes prepared by B. Max Mehl (to cite just one person), our staff experts have found that what was called "Uncirculated" years ago is, in numerous instances, just Extremely Fine or AU by today's American Numismatic Association or *Photograde* standards. It was not that the old-time numismatists intended to deceive anyone. The situation is that the emphasis placed on grading accuracy today simply was not present years ago. Even within the realm of my own experience I can recall—and this is verified by our firm's catalogues

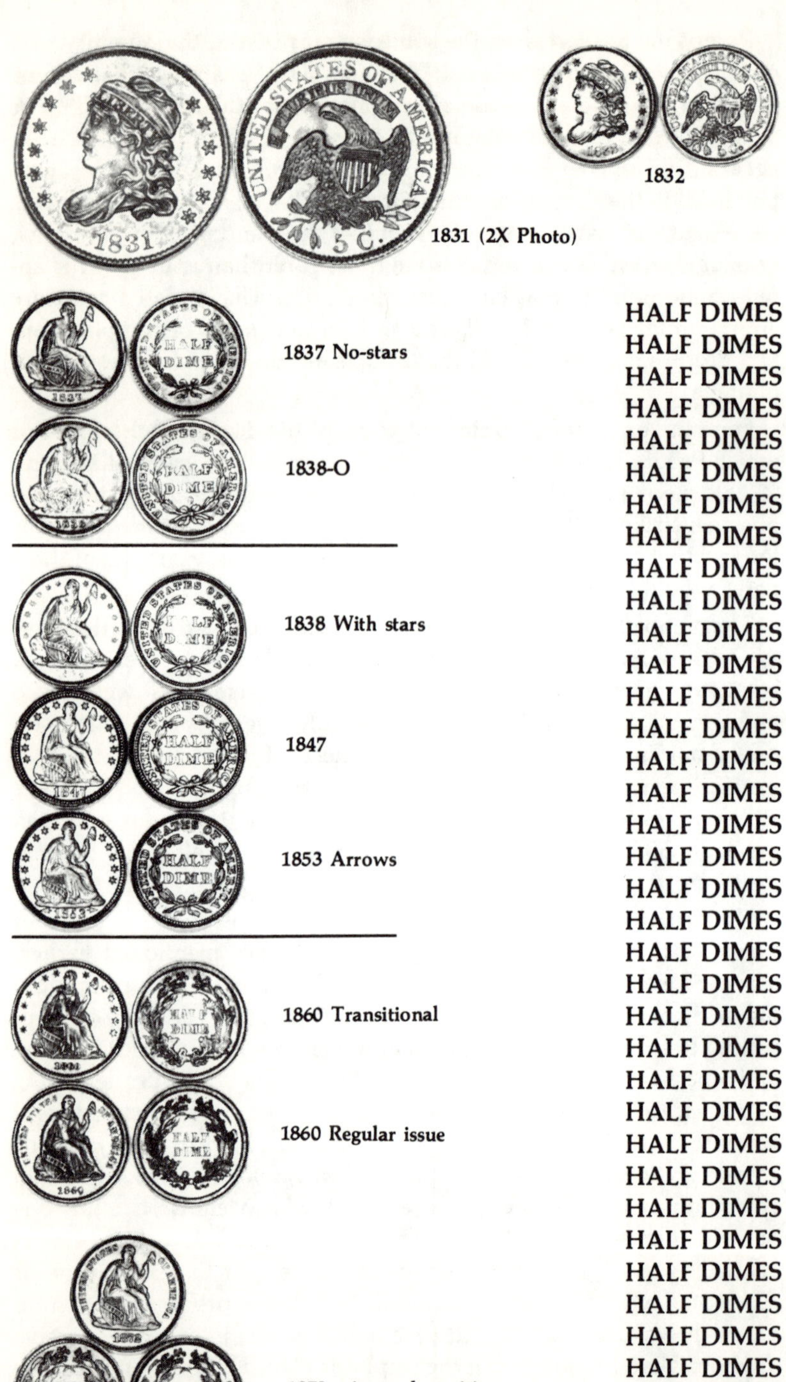

1831 (2X Photo)

1832

1837 No-stars

1838-O

1838 With stars

1847

1853 Arrows

1860 Transitional

1860 Regular issue

1872 mintmark positions

from 20 or 30 years ago—that either a coin was considered Uncirculated or it wasn't. Such gradations as MS-60, MS-63, MS-65, MS-67, and MS-70, if used, would have had collectors and dealers alike rolling in the aisles with laughter! No one particularly cared. Reading even earlier numismatic periodicals issued by different professional numismatists will show that especially scarce pieces often were graded higher. Thus, such notations as "Uncirculated *for the coin*" were applied to 1793 large cents, early gold pieces and the like; for coins which today might grade only Extremely Fine.

The summation of all of this is that one can't scan auction catalogues and price lists of decades ago and conclude, for example, that 1838-O half dimes or 1838-O dimes in Uncirculated condition exist to the extent of perhaps several dozen pieces each. However, examination *in person* of these same coins, when their pedigrees can be traced today, will reveal that many of yesteryear's Uncirculated coins would be called Extremely Fine or AU today.

This has a significance for today's collector. Many catalogue listings are very casual. They assume that Uncirculated pieces are readily available. Certain *great rarities* are listed at relatively low figures in Uncirculated grade.

The preceding words are a desirable preface to half dimes and to other early American silver and gold coins in general. Time and time again I will refer to a given issue as being *rare*, but a perusal of popular reference books will not indicate a sky-high price. This is not contradictory. It is just that the rarity of numerous early issues has not been recognized by the marketplace.

The Liberty Seated design was modified in 1838. A semicircle of 13 stars was added around the obverse border. This general design was used in the half dime series from 1838 through 1859.

Early pieces in the series lack drapery at Miss Liberty's elbow. Mint officials decided that this was an oversight and agreed that the addition of drapery would make Miss Liberty's dress more flowing in appearance. So, this feature became a part of all denominations featuring the Liberty Seated design. The proportional size of the drapery differed vastly from one series to another. On the half dimes of 1840 the drapery is very large. On Liberty Seated half dollars it is very small in proportion.

From 1838 through 1853 Liberty Seated half dimes were produced at the Philadelphia and New Orleans mints. The New Orleans issues bear distinctive O mintmarks.

Many varieties of half dimes occur throughout the 1837-1873 period, including the 1849/6 and 1849/8 overdates. A number of pieces are elusive, 1846 being the most prominent Philadelphia Mint date in this regard. In general, New Orleans half dimes of this period are quite rare in Uncirculated grade. These have been grossly undervalued and unappreciated over the years. The 1849-O half dime is elusive in all conditions, and a Choice Uncirculated coin, if one ever appears on the auction market, would be a cause for celebration among half dime specialists!

In 1853 tiny arrowheads were added to half dimes alongside the date. This was to signify a reduction in the weight of the pieces. The price of silver was rising during this period, so the official weights of coins were reduced to prevent pieces from being melted down for bullion value. These arrows were continued on half dimes through 1855. While most with-arrows issues were minted in large quantities (1855-O being an exception), prices are generally higher for pieces of this design as examples are in strong demand for inclusion in type sets. A major scarcity is the 1853-O without arrows issue, a coin produced early in the 1853 year.

In 1856 the arrows were discontinued. The earlier design was resumed from that point until 1859. The 1856-1859 span includes two interesting varieties, one of which is very rare. The first is the seldom seen 1858 half dime with regular date over inverted date. The engraver first cut the entire date 1858 upside-down. Realizing his error, he then punched the date in its correct position. A magnifying glass clearly shows both sets of numerals. This issue is scarce in all grades and is a major rarity in Uncirculated preservation.

In my *Coin World* "Numismatic Depth Study" column I had the honor of first publicizing this variety to the numismatic fraternity (over the years similar pleasures were had by being the first to publish the 1938-D/S overmintmark nickel and several other previously unknown pieces). First, one 1858 inverted date half dime was identified, then a few more, then, as collectors all over the United States began checking their pieces, still others turned up. It is probably accurate to say that more than a hundred pieces exist today, including three or four in Mint State. Still, as noted, the piece is rare.

The second interesting variety is the 1859 Philadelphia Mint half dime with stars having hollow center points. All 1859 half dimes have this feature. What constitutes a "type" and what doesn't is a matter of opinion. While tradition has not dictated that the 1859 half dime be isolated as a specific piece needed for type sets, still it is interesting and distinctive.

In 1859 and 1860 two transitional pattern half dime varieties were made. Each of these is interesting inasmuch as the term UNITED STATES OF AMERICA does not appear on either. The obverse of each features the Liberty Seated design with stars surrounding. The reverse features the notation HALF DIME surrounded by a wreath. The 1859 issue is extremely rare, and often a period of years will pass between auction offerings. The 1860 transitional pattern half dime was minted to the extent of 100 pieces, according to a personal notebook kept by James Ross Snowden, Mint director at the time. This mintage figure should probably be taken with a grain of salt, for my firm has had nearly this many over the years, and other firms have handled additional pieces. In 1973, when writing an article on this issue, I noted that as of that time we had handled approximately 50 pieces, and since that time more have gone through our hands. Specimens of this issue were struck with frosty "Uncirculated" surfaces, rather than Proof finish, an unusual situation for a pattern. When encountered, specimens of the 1860 transitional are apt to be in frosty, Choice Uncirculated grade. I have never seen one with even a slight degree of wear.

In 1860 the regular half dime design was changed. The stars on the obverse were replaced by the inscription UNITED STATES OF AMERICA. The reverse wreath was changed to a larger and bulkier style. Half dimes of this design were made from 1860 through 1873 inclusive.

Among these later half dimes are several scarce varieties, including Philadelphia Mint issues 1863 through 1867 inclusive. San Francisco Mint coins of the period 1863-1869 are quite scarce in higher grades. Among San Francisco coins of the 1860s and early 1870s are numerous pieces which have the Liberty Seated figure on the obverse engraved, as if by a scraping tool. Obviously an attempt was made to shave off silver from the figure, but this was done by following the contours of the Liberty Seated figure so as not to make the removal obvious except upon close inspection. Examples showing this are sufficiently common that there must have been a widespread reason for doing this. Probably the explanation is that these pieces were exported in quantity to the Orient, and silver was shaved off by various merchants there who desired to amass silver on a bit by bit basis. A flaw in this theory is that trade dollars, which were circulated in large quantities in the Orient at the same time, rarely show this feature. Certain of these scraped half dimes show button shanks mounted on the back, another mystery. The writer once purchased a small group of about 200 San Francisco half dimes of this era, and each had the scraped feature.

One of the most marvelous numismatic discoveries in recent decades is the 1870-S half dime. Prior to a few years ago no one dreamed that an 1870-S half dime existed. Indeed, no such coin is mentioned in the Mint reports. Apparently sloppy records were kept in San Francisco in 1870, for there is no mintage record of the 1870-S silver dollar either, and yet a number of such dollars exist (and are great rarities). Rarcoa, the Chicago firm, dazzled the hobby in the 1970s by announcing that

UNIQUE 1870-S HALF DIME

One of the greatest finds in modern times is this 1870-S half dime. Previously unknown, the 1870-S came to light in 1978 when it was displayed by Rarcoa, a Chicago dealer. An article in "Numismatic News," May 10, 1980, told of the sale of the piece:

"A unique 1870-S half dime discovered in 1978 has been sold by Rarcoa for $425,000 to John Abbott, a Michigan coin dealer. Abbott said that he had been 'trying to buy it for quite some time,' but not at the $500,000 price Edward Milas, Rarcoa president was asking. 'We made an agreement to buy it at $25,000 over what the 1804 silver dollar brought at the recent Garrett Collection auction,' Abbott explained. 'That's how we reached a price on it,' he continued.

The circumstances surrounding the striking of the 1870-S dime are not known. Produced during the first year of the San Francisco Mint, it may have been made simply to test the dies or as part of a presentation set or group to an important official.

an 1870-S half dime had come to light. The piece was exhibited at several conventions. I had the privilege of examining it closely. The piece, being a new discovery, had not been publicized earlier and was not famous. However, such fame will surely come. The unique 1870-S half dime was sold to John Abbott, the well-known Michigan professional numismatist. Secretly I wished that it had been consigned to one of our auction sales instead, for it would have been interesting to have researched the piece in detail and to have presented it in a multiple-page spread.

The selling price of $425,000 for the piece, as subsequently reported in *A Guide Book of United States Coins*, was said to have been derived in an unusual manner. What is the coin worth? The thought went through the minds of Ed Milas and Dennis Forgue, the owners of Rarcoa. It was decided that when my firm auctioned the Garrett Collection 1804 silver dollar as part of a series of sales we were conducting for The Johns Hopkins University, the selling price of this famous rarity, plus $25,000, would be a reasonable figure for the unique 1870-S. In a fantastic "fight" among enthusiastic bidders on the auction floor, the 1804 silver dollar broke all past records and soared to $400,000, thus setting the auction sale record for any United States silver coin! As agreed beforehand, $25,000 was added to the price, and $425,000 became the transaction basis for the 1870-S half dime.

In 1872 two half dime varieties were created at the San Francisco Mint, one with a mintmark above the wreath bow and the other with a mintmark below. The year 1873 saw several series end their existence. Not only did production of the half dime end, but two-cent pieces and silver three-cent pieces were discontinued as well.

During the last decade or so of the half dime denomination pieces were not released into circulation at the time of coinage but were stored by the Treasury. During the period specie payments were suspended, and silver coins did not circulate. The gap was filled by nickel five-cent pieces of the same value.

Worn and Proof half dimes of the type from 1860 through the end of the series in 1873 are available in proportion to their original mintages. Pieces from the Philadelphia Mint from 1863 through 1867 in particular are elusive. Higher mintages were recorded for the San Francisco emissions. While numerous examples were stored by the Treasury Department during the specie payment suspension years, it is probable that a good share of them were sent overseas in payment for various supplies. This would explain the earlier-mentioned pieces which presumably were engraved in the Orient.

So far as Uncirculated pieces are concerned, those most often seen of the 1860-1873 type are 1861 and 1862 Philadelphia as well as 1871, 1872, 1872-S, 1873, and 1873-S.

Collecting Liberty Seated half dimes by date affords an interesting possibility. While no numismatist has ever put together a complete set of Uncirculated and Proof issues, and while such probably never will be done, it is possible to assemble a group in lesser grades, possibly spiced with Proof and Uncirculated pieces of later years. This discussion does not include the unique 1870-S which has to be, as Dr. Sheldon called certain large cents which were virtually unobtainable, "non-collectible." It is financially within the reach of many to use the grades Fine to Extremely Fine as an objective and to get one each of every issue 1837 and later.

A group, the Liberty Seated Coin Club, exists for the benefit of those interested in the various silver denominations bearing this design. Variations in mintmark placement, observations concerning rarity, and other facets are objects of articles and discussions in their periodical, *The Gobrecht Journal.*

What constitutes a "type" among Liberty Seated coins admits of no precise definition. As noted earlier, the 1859 half dime, the unique year with the stars hollow in the center, is not generally considered to be a type. Most numismatists assembling a comprehensive set include the following: Type of 1837 and 1838-O without obverse stars; type of 1838 to 1853, and again from 1856 through 1859, with stars on the obverse and UNITED STATES OF AMERICA on the reverse; type of 1853-1855 as preceding but with arrowheads alongside the date; and type of 1860-1873 with UNITED STATES OF AMERICA on the obverse.

The preceding "standard" types can be refined by including the issues of 1838-1840 without drapery at the elbow and/or the much-discussed (by me; others seem to ignore it) 1859 with hollow stars. The 1859 and 1860 issues without UNITED STATES OF AMERICA on either obverse or reverse are transitional patterns, not regular issues, and are generally not included.

It is appropriate to close my discussion of half dimes with some remarks made by a connoisseur of the series, Dr. W.E. Caldwell of Baldwyn, Mississippi. In November 1973 I had the pleasure of cataloguing his outstanding collection and presenting it for auction sale. In connection with this, Dr. Caldwell sent a few paragraphs concerning his coins and the enthusiasm with which he collected them. I quote from his notes:

"It has been a pleasure to collect the half dimes which you will be selling in your November auction. My collecting of this series began quite by accident. I was convalescing from a heart attack when my maid brought in some old coins to see if they were valuable. I laid my paintbrushes (my hobby to this point) aside, thank goodness, and borrowed a friend's *Guide Book of United States Coins.*

"I evaluated the small group of miscellaneous coins and bought them. Among these pieces was a well-worn 1837 Liberty Seated half dime which had been holed and plugged. This tiny coin brought back memories of an elderly uncle who gave me a nickel for the local Saturday Opera House movies each week when I was a child. I remember that many of these 'nickels' were half dimes. Why not collect half dimes and see how many different dates I could find? An interesting idea!

"Soon I was off and running—buying half dimes wherever I could find them. One can 'buy in haste and repent in leisure,' and after a few months of fast spending I was many dollars wiser! I found it was desirable to buy from reputable dealers, large auction houses, and at major conventions. It seemed that by this method I could be more sure of getting a quality coin even though a premium price might be required. The you get what you pay for' adage is certainly true, and I found this out!

"My collection begins with a 1792 half disme, a coin which certainly is one of the most romantic issues in American numismatics. At one time I had a specimen of each and every half dime variety from 1792 to 1873, but later I traded or sold some of the very worn pieces in the hope that I would be able to get top grade pieces later. It turned out that I was able to do this in some instances but not in others. It is very, very difficult to obtain true Uncirculated examples of the 1794-1805 years, and had this been an absolute requirement there would have been many dates which I would never have acquired. I feel that all Uncirculated half dimes of this era are grossly undervalued, and that examples in grades close to this grade are of extreme rarity in many instances.

"Among the 1829-1837 Capped Bust half dimes you might find it interesting to know that the 1836 Small 5c and the 1837 Small 5c varieties are much, much rarer in Uncirculated grades than catalogues indicate. The 1838-O of the Liberty Seated without-stars type is also very undervalued. The specimen that you will be auctioning is the finest I have been able to buy in five years of searching. [Note: I graded the coin AU in the catalogue.]

"Among later Liberty Seated half dimes there are many rarities, particularly in the New Orleans pieces. Many if not most New Orleans half dimes are very weakly struck on the reverse, and to find a sharp strike, if indeed this is possible at all, many specimens must be examined. The most underrated seem to be the 1840-O without drapery, the 1842-O, and the 1844-O. The 1846 Philadelphia Mint half dime is exceedingly rare in higher grades. Another sleeper is the 1848 Large Date in mint condition. Major rarities are 1849-O, 1852-O, and 1853-O without arrows in better grades.

"A very interesting issue is the 1858. You will note that I purchased several examples of this date in order to study them. There is the 'regular' date, the inverted date, and the doubled date—and I suspect that some of these may be different states of the same original die.

"The 1859 transitional issue with the reverse of 1860 must rate as one of the most important of all American coin rarities. During the period I formed my collection, the present specimen, the one you will be auctioning, is the only one I was able to buy, and no others were offered for sale in price lists or auctions.

"Finally, the 1869-S is an overlooked regular issue. I was only able to find a few Uncirculated pieces offered for sale, despite the fact that the catalogues treat this as a 'common date.'

"All pattern half dimes are scarce, and most are rare. The 1794 copper half dime has been the highlight of my patterns.

"I can close my eyes and see all of the half dimes in my collection. I hope that the successful bidders on the individual lots will experience the same pleasure I did from these beautiful pieces. While a monetary profit will undoubtedly be realized on the collection, I have profited in what is perhaps an even better way: five years of enjoyable collecting."

Nickel Miscellany

or, What a Nickel Could Do

During the 'teens the nickel was the passport to entertainment at the movies. Typically, one could pay the admission charge and stay all day if desired—watching a succession of one- and two-reel films. Such places were called nickelodeon theaters, the nickel part of the term derived from the admission charge and odeon being the Greek word for theater.

PUT ANOTHER NICKEL IN

Or, What Melodies a Nickel Could Produce In 1916!

Back in 1916 a nickel was the passport to all sorts of pleasures. Far from being an unnoticed piece of little value, a nickel was important. It could stand on its own. It could buy a glass of beer, it could pay the admission charge to see Charlie Chaplin on the silver screen, or it could buy a ticket on a merry-go-round. Or, if you happened to be at the Shanghai Cafe in downtown Minneapolis, it could buy you a concert, for there larger than life was a wonderous device called a Wurlitzer Mandolin PianOrchestra, to be technical a Style 16. Made in the Rudolph Wurlitzer plant in North Tonawanda, New York, the unit was shipped west and installed in what certainly must have been one of the most curious eateries of its time. Amidst indoor trees and potted plants live canaries flew among the branches, hopefully without alighting on the throngs who crowded the place most evenings.

Perhaps the owner of the Shanghai Cafe was attracted by an advertisement which proclaimed:

"The perfect rendering of music by mechanical means is one of the problems that has taxed human ingenuity since the first appearance of the time-honored hand-organ. The many efforts made in this direction, although meritorious, have heretofore failed to reproduce the composition as executed by the players. In the latest invention, the PianOrchestra, the hearer receives the same impression as if the performance were given by regular musicians. There is the same volume, technique and expression, conveying to the ear a perfect musical sensation.

"The cases in which the instruments of the PianOrchestra are set are artistic in design and would be an ornament wherever placed. They are composed of oak, and throughout both material and workmanship will bear the closest inspection. The mechanism is promptly and conveniently regulated by electricity. The rolls of music, each containing from four to six pieces, making a concert of about 20 minutes per roll, work automatically on steel rollers. When run to the end the roll rewinds itself, and, unless stopped, the performance of itself begins anew.

"Where music lovers congregate, as in resorts, beer gardens, hotels, cafes, saloons and in homes, the PianOrchestra is proving itself indispensable. It is impossible to do justice to these magnificent musical structures by pen descriptions; to be admired and appreciated they must be seen and heard!

"In the PianOrchestra the fact is established that it is possible to furnish the highest musical enjoyment at a minute's notice. The program, including the production of the best composers of two hemispheres, is always prepared. Simply by touching an electric button the mechanism is put into motion and the apartment is flooded either with the divine strains of a Beethoven sonata, a Mendelssohn nocturne, a Strauss waltz or a Wagner opera, alternating at will with airs and melodies of a lighter vein, but equally all enjoyable and edifying...

"For hotels, larger cafes, beer gardens, dancing pavilions, ice cream parlors, penny arcades, five-cent theatres, and similar amusement resorts, there is nothing to equal that PianOrchestra as an attraction and money-maker. In large public resorts, where a number of slot boxes can be distributed about the place, connecting with the instrument, so that it may be played from any part of the house by dropping a five-cent piece, the PianOrchestra will take in its cost in nickels within a year or so, besides doubling the volume of business."

As it happened, the Style 16 PianOrchestra and a nice supply of music rolls cost the owner just over $2200. Weighing close to a ton, it stood about nine feet high and contained a variety of automatically-played instruments: piano, organ pipes representing violin and violoncello, chimes or orchestra bells, bass drum, snare drum, kettle drum effect, xylophone, triangle, tambourine, and castanets.

Oswald Wurdeman, who used to sell and service automatic musical instruments in Minneapolis and who in the 1960s, just before he died, furnished much historical information to the present writer, reminisced about the Style 16:

"It's hard for me to remember the different Wurlitzer models, but I do recall the Style 16 PianOrchestra. What an orchestrion it was! You would put a nickel in it and it would light up like a Christmas tree! There were two of them in Minneapolis. One was in a restaurant, the Shanghai Cafe, downtown. I used to service it. The Shanghai was like something out of a fairy tale, all in the Oriental style. The inside of the place was full of carved teak furniture, vases, live trees, and other decorations. Birds flew around in the air as you ate dinner. It was quite an attraction at one time, although not many remember it now. The orchestrion later went to the Stagecoach Inn in Shakopee, not far from Minneapolis. Perhaps you've seen it there... Rolls were very important. You had to have the right kind of music [on the paper music rolls which contained the program for the instrument]. Mostly the people liked the new music they heard when shows came to town or on phonograph records. This was before the radio was popular. I used to tell the owners to throw away the rolls after a few months, except for certain songs which were old favorites and were always popular. I made a lot of money selling rolls."

The nickel was king of the entertainment business in 1916, and while the Wurlitzer PianOrchestra was gathering a silver-colored stream of them in the Shanghai Cafe, thousands of other coin-operated pianos were taking in their share in locations ranging from bowling alleys to bordellos, from restaurants to roadside stops.

Wurlitzer Mandolin PianOrchestra—Style 16

With Wurlitzer Automatic Roll Changer

The art glass designs vary somewhat.

Instrumentation:

Piano — Orchestration of 42 Violin and Violoncello Pipes
Chimes — Bass, Snare and Kettle Drums
Xylophone — Triangle Tambourine Castanets

Height over all, 8 ft. 8 in. Height without Globes, 7 ft. 10 in. Width, 5 ft. 10½ in. Depth, 2 ft. 11 in. Shipping weight, 1600 lbs.

While Wurlitzer was the acknowledged giant of the industry, out in Chicago the J.P. Seeburg Piano Co. was achieving a grand measure of success with its Style G and H orchestrions and other products, the Style H being richly ornamented with two carved statues, many panels of art glass, and three hanging lamps. Drop a nickel in the slot, and a jazz band came to life. Two minutes later all was silent, and another nickel was required to liven the scene once again. The Operators' Piano Company and the Marquette Piano Company, also in Chicago, did a lively trade, as did Peerless (in St. Johnsville, New York), Link in Binghamton, New York, and numerous others. Across the sea in Germany, Ludwig Hupfeld, the world's largest manufacturer of automatic musical instruments, kept nearly 6,000 pairs of hands busy at one point turning out devices from compact player pianos to gigantic orchestrions, some of which sold for more than $10,000 each. One of the most remarkable mechanical contrivances mankind has ever known was the Hupfeld Phonoliszt-Violina, which reproduced the playing of a violinist with piano accompaniment. Fortunately for collectors, of the thousands originally produced probably 50 or more still exist today.

As incredible as it may seem, it was possible to spend several thousand dollars for a nickel-operated orchestrion and to recoup one's investment within two or three years. Many such machines were kept busy from morning until night. The total amount of wealth that could be accumulated by amassing nickels was not lost to advertisers of such devices, for Link noted that Woolworth first proved that "20 nickels make a dollar, you know!" And, "when dollars are hard to get, go after profitable nickels." Considering the thousands of coin-operated pianos and orchestrions once in use, it is probably accurate to say that any well-worn Shield, Liberty or early Buffalo nickel in existence today has passed through the coin slots of many such instruments, perhaps hundreds of times. Indeed, their voracious appetite for nickels later caused the public to refer to such machines as "nickelodeons," although in their original time of use they were given the more lofty "automatic piano" designation by the trade. Similarly, when the jukebox became popular in the 1930s, the manufacturers disliked this slang term and preferred to call them "automatic phonographs." Finally, Wurlitzer yielded on the subject, and their last production, made in 1972 right before the North Tonawanda factory closed down, bears the prominent inscription JUKEBOX on the front!

Curiously, a nickel was the price paid for hearing a tune when the first coin-operated piano appeared on the American scene in 1898. As recently as the 1960s, over a half century later, a nickel would also buy you a tune—perhaps a vocal by Elvis Presley—in a jukebox, this despite raging inflation in just about every other area of human endeavor.

From 1898 until around 1910, nickel-operated, hand-cranked music boxes such as this Regina model were familiar sights in soda parlors, saloons, restaurants, and other places of public amusements. Twelve metal discs, each measuring 27 inches in diameter, were stored in a rack, like pieces of bread in a toaster. Each time a nickel was deposited, a new tune would play. Or, if desired, a pointer on the right side of the unit could be set to play a particular tune on the program. (Instrument from the Pugsley Collection illustrated in "Music Machines, American Style," Smithsonian Institution, 1971).

The Tiny Coinola

With Xylophones.

Compact fits any place and is a **Money Mint.**

50 cents worth of electricity collects $100.00 in Nickels.

Tiny Coinola Xylophone

Height 55" **Width 36"** **Depth 21"**

Piano---Mandolin---Xylophones uses regular A or 65 note roll.

A proven earning capacity equal to any big piano.

Costs less than any piano on the market and gives far more.

Will put NEW LIFE in business.

The Operators' Paino Co.

"Pianos that Pay"

715 North Kedzie Avenue

Chicago, Illinois

The Duplex Midget

(The latest Coinola)

So unusual it commands instant attention

So novel they will keep it playing all the time.

Duplex Interior.

The best money maker out.

Two rolls, the choice of selections and always ready for more use.

Catalogs and Prices on request to Dealers in open territory.

Coinola Dealers are always busy

There's a real reason---

COINOLAS.

"50 cents worth of electricity collects $100.00 in nickels," proclaims the copy in an advertisement for a Coinola nickel-operated piano made in Chicago. This compact unit, consisting of an automatically-played piano with mandolin attachment and xylophone accompaniment, was described as a "money mint," as indeed it probably was.

The Operators' Piano Company, Chicago, was one of more than a dozen American firms engaged in the manufacture of coin-operated pianos and their larger cousins, orchestrions (automatic orchestras). Often costing $1,000 to $2,000 or more, it was not unusual for such devices to repay their cost via the nickel slot within several years!

(From "Player Piano Treasury" by Harvey N. Roehl, as are several of the other musical illustrations shown here)

FOR SALE ON EASY TERMS

BY THE

AUTOMATIC . MUSICAL . . COMPANY .

53 CHENANGO ST., BINGHAMTON, N. Y.

Among the most curious of all nickel-operated pianos was the Encore Automatic Banjo. This 1903 advertisement is by the Automatic Musical Company, Binghamton, New York, a distributor. By means of a perforated paper roll, the Encore automatically played each of the four banjo strings and provided the listener with a snappy tune each time a nickel was deposited.

It's LITTLE Nickels, LARGELY Profit, That Count Toward DIVIDEND Dollars

WOOLWORTH first proved the possibilities of PROFITABLE Nickel Sales.

Nickels collected in a Link Automatic Piano will bring the proof HOME to you! They are 99% profit.

And a Link gives your Customer his money's worth! It plays excellent music to perfect dance time, requires no attention, plays from endless music rolls that do not repeat for half an hour. It attracts patrons and will substantially add to your profits.

If dollars are hard to get—

GO AFTER PROFITABLE NICKELS

with a

Link Piano

You'll find they soon amount to DOLLARS OF PROFIT.

A Link gathers in nickels that are 99 per cent. profit, yet amply repays its customers with the latest popular music, excellently played to perfect dance time.

It quickly repays the initial investment necessary. These nickels likewise result, indirectly, in increased merchandise sales and lend to your store an atmosphere of activity and prosperity.

Send the coupon below if you desire additional information. Ask us anything you would like to know in regard to our proposition, price, terms, etc. Tell us what kind of business you are in and if we believe a "Link" would prove a money-maker there, we'll prove it by offering you most liberal payment terms.

Tell me what profits LINK PIANOS are making in business places similar to mine. Also send prices and best terms.

....

....

....

YOUR NAME ....

ADDRESS ....

LINE OF BUSINESS ....

The Link Piano Company, Binghamton, New York (successors to the Automatic Musical Company), noted the power of the nickel: "It's little nickels, largely profit, that count toward dividend dollars," "Woolworths first proved the possibilities of profitable nickel sales," "Nickels collected in a Link Automatic Piano will bring the proof home to you! They are 99% profit," and "If dollars are hard to get, go after profitable nickels... You'll find they soon amount to dollars of profit."

It is a strange footnote to American business history to mention that the Link Piano Company, which later made aviation trainers (today the Link name is well known for flight trainers and simulators) had its beginnings in the same building on Water Street, Binghamton, as did the International Time Recorder Company, which later became IBM!

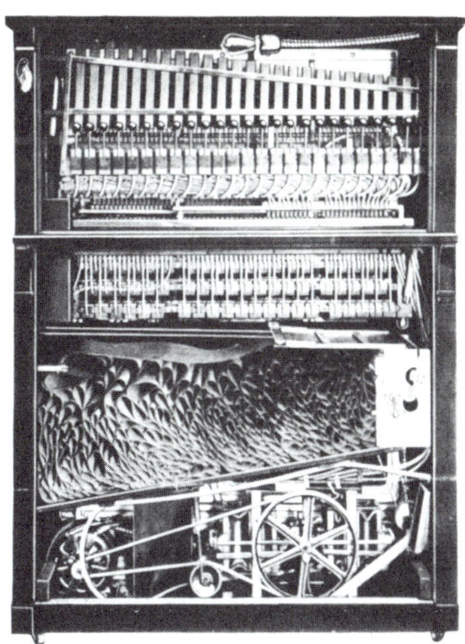

Style 2 -- E

Piano -- Mandolin -- Marimbaphone

No Rewinding No Pauses The Link is played by an endless music roll on which are fifteen pieces of popular dance music. As patrons drop nickels these pieces are played in rotation. No adjustment, no rewinding, is necessary. The same selection is not repeated for half an hour. Each roll contains enough music so that it need not be changed as often as on other makes of instruments.

15 Popular Pieces on Each Endless Roll Each nickel dropped in a Link brings full value of snappy music, accurately timed, perfectly accented, "full of pep," contagious with entertainment. Only pieces that have proved themselves hits in New York and Chicago are cut into Link rolls and fifteen on one endless roll. Each piece invites the listener to hear the next. Each adds life and high spirits to the store—and profits to the bank roll.

Probably the most popular Link piano was the Style 2-E which featured an endless-type paper roll and played a piano, mandolin, and marimbaphone (xylophone). "Each nickel dropped in a Link brings full value of snappy music, accurately timed, perfectly accented, full of pep, contagious with entertainment," the copy notes. Indeed, the Link empire was built upon the lowly nickel, as were the empires of Woolworth, Coca-Cola, Moxie, Wrigley, and numerous others. It would be an interesting exercise to add up the number of nickels minted prior to, say, 1920 and correlate this with the estimated annual sales of firms which made products which sold for a nickel. The result would undoubtedly show that the typical nickel never stopped moving from place to place!

Providence, R. I., February 20th, 1912

Gentlemen: We are shipping four **Pianolins** to Hartford, Conn. this week and wish we had about ten more of them, as we think the **Pianolin** is the best automatic instrument in the market for operating.

We believe that they get more money than any other small piano we have ever seen and that they are also very reliable as automatic machines of this kind go and we congratulate you on producing such a successful machine.

Thanking you very much for past favors shown us and with kindest regards to all, beg to remain,

Yours very truly,
NEW ENGLAND
AUTOMATIC AMUSEMENT CO.
Per. L. F. N. Baldwin

Pianolin

Clarksville, Tex.,
Feb. 20th, 1912

Gentlemen: Several months ago I purchased a **Pianolin** and I notice by the card inclosed that you make the music for it. I would like a catalogue of all of the music you have. This instrument plays such perfect time that I believe it will be fine to dance by and would like music for such occasions.

Very truly yours,

J. H. BURTON,
Lyric Theatre

Crown Candy Kitchen

Collingwood, Ont., July 12th, 1910

Gentlemen: We are very much pleased with our **Pianolin,** and wish to say, that it has already paid for itself in the increased business it has brought us since we installed it last April. The people here are very fond of it, and we all think it the best instrument for the money in the world.

C. GEORGAS, Prop.
Pianolin.

Grand Rapids, Mich.,
July 19th, 1910

Gentlemen: I received the **Pianolin** on Friday afternoon, and by 5.30 P. M. it was working fine. It is a splendid instrument, and I am pleased with it. My friends say that the music is the very best they have ever heard on an instrument of the size. We counted the cash it has taken since Friday (4 days) and it amounted to $31.65. It has also helped the bar trade wonderfully, and I would not part with it for the best electric piano on the market. Thanking you for all past favors, I remain,

Pianolin "A"

Respectfully yours,

BERT WOSINSKI

Tonawanda, N. Y., August 31st, 1910

Gentlemen: My Pianolin is doing great work, as it is averaging over $100.00 per month, and it has increased my bar trade from $5.00 to $8.00 per day, and I would not take twice what I paid for it if I could not get another one of them.

Respectfully yours,

WILLIAM KOLPACK

Orchestrina

Sacramento, Cal.
July 2nd, 1911

Dear Sir: I have purchased an **Orchestrina** recently for my Moving Picture House here in Sacramento. This is what I believe the largest instrument you manufacture, and I want to tell you gentlemen, that it is the most wonderful musical contrivance that I have ever heard in my life, and it pleases my patrons.

I would like to give you a standing order for five or six rolls of music a month, of the latest popular music.

Yours very truly,
C. W. GODARD,
Acme Theatre, Sacramento, Cal.

FERGUSON MUSIC COMPANY,
Southern Agents
514 W. Forsyth Street

Jacksonville, Fla., March 24th, 1912

Gentlemen: Since writing you, I have received two 44 note Pianos of different makes, and have put them right alongside of yours, and it doesn't take an expert to see which one is the best.

I have been in the automatic piano business for a number of years, and for the money, I must say, that you have the best little instrument I have ever heard, and I want to congratulate you on this Piano, as it is very simple, and the music is good.

I hope that you will get me off the six at once, and I assure you this state will be worked, and worked hard, as I am simply daffy about this little Piano.

Hoping that you will get the Pianos off right away, I remain as ever, your friend.

THE FERGUSON MUSIC CO.
By Wm. L. Hackney

Pianolin "B"

Olcott, N. Y., July 20th, 1911

Dear Sir: Kindly send to the appended address, roll No. 467, and inclosed is check covering same. The instrument is working fine and giving good results.

Very truly yours,
Pianolin SAMUEL MEYER, Park View Hotel

Sextrola Style "B"

Manufactured by

NORTH TONAWANDA MUSICAL INSTRUMENT WORKS

North Tonawanda, N. Y., U. S. A.

The coin-operated pianos showed on this page all were nickel-in-the-slot devices. It was not unusual for such an instrument to pay for itself within a year or two via the nickels deposited in the slot. Indeed, one of the testimonials printed above tells of $31.65 received in just four days.

Wilcoxson & Swingley's Confectionery Store
Livingston, Mont.

VIOLANO-VIRTUOSO

Manufactured by

MILLS NOVELTY COMPANY, Chicago

The Violano-Virtuoso consisted of a real violin and piano automatically played by an ingenious system of electromagnets. The program of five tunes was on a perforated paper roll, somewhat like a home player piano roll but more sophisticated. Approximately 5,000 of these violin players were sold from around 1910 to 1930. On this and the next several pages are shown Violano-Virtuoso units on location as illustrated in a Mills publicity booklet of the 1920s. Each Violano-Virtuoso was hungry for nickels, and if the testimonials are to be believed, the typical unit gobbled them up at a frightening rate!

NEW NORTH END HOTEL

New York, N. Y.

HOTEL HOWE

Akron, Ohio

Mills Novelty Co.,
Jackson Blvd. & Green St.,
Chicago, Ill.

Gentlemen:-

In regard to our VIOLANO VIRTUOSO, of which we sent you a photograph the other day, we are more than pleased with it, and have been ever since its installation, about eight months ago. We do not give people much chance to drop in nickels, as we use it instead of an orchestra for our dining room. It takes the place of music which was costing us $50.00 per week. Still, at that, the receipts from it are sufficient to pay for new music rolls and supplies.

As a wonderful invention, it calls forth a great deal of comment, and is very frequently taken for an orchestra.

We would not be without it and look upon it as a first-class investment, having given excellent satisfaction from the start. We are very glad to recommend it to anyone in our line of business.

Thanking you for the excellent service you have given us on the instrument, we are,

Cordially yours,

HOTEL HOWE COMPANY.

F. S. Ozier

PRES.

COHAN'S GRAND OPERA HOUSE

CHICAGO, ILL.

Mr. H. S. Mills,
Pres. Mills Novelty Co.
Chicago, Ills.

Dear Sir:

The Automatic Violin is a wonderful invention and I heartily congratulate you and really feel that it will prove a great success. The first time I heard it playing my song ''The Grand Old Flag'' I rushed to make the acquaintance of so fine a soloist and discovered this marvelous piece of machinery.

Good luck to it and its promoters.

Geo. M. Cohan

DEMOS BROTHERS

Kenosha, Wis.

VIOLANO-VIRTUOSO

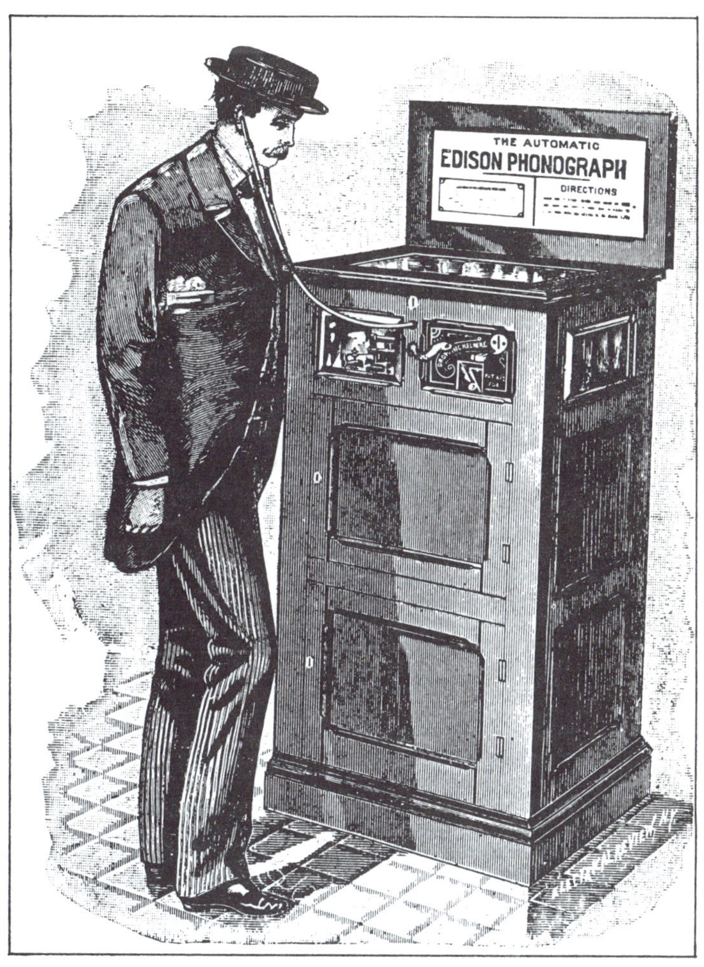

During the 1890s Thomas Edison manufactured large quantities of coin-operated phonographs. Indeed, he envisioned the phonograph (which he invented in 1877) to be mainly a commercial item suitable for the office (for dictating) or for coin-operated use. He down played any suggestion that millions citizens across the United States would someday desire them in their homes. Equipped to take nickels or cents, primarily nickels, such devices were often arrayed in long rows in what became known as "phonograph parlors." New York, Chicago, San Francisco, and other large metropolitan centers boasted multiple establishments which drew hundreds of patrons each day. (Illustration from "The Phonogram," February 1891, as reproduced in "Music Machines American Style," Smithsonian Institution, 1971).

REGINA
HEXAPHONE
5c

The Regina Music Box Company of Rahway, New Jersey, produced approximately 100,000 music boxes, many of which were nickel-operated, from the 1890s until shortly before 1920. After the turn of the century, Regina realized that the newfangled phonograph was gaining an important share of the market, so it introduced the hexaphone, a nickel-operated windup phonograph which stored six cylinder records. The patron was free to choose any tune on the program. Here was the forerunner of what later was to be known as the jukebox. However, during the several years before 1910, when the Hexaphone was in its ascendancy, no one dreamed that within two decades music boxes would be collectors items and cylinder phonogrph would be rapidly heading in that direction, to be replaced by disc-type records.

The nickel was the basic coin used in automatic phonogrpahs and pianos. Virtually any worn nickel from the late nineteenth or early twentieth century has probably seen hundreds of trips through the coin slots of such devices.

Mills Roulette..Seven-Way..Front View

The dial has eighty spaces. This machine pays from 10 cents to $2.00 when played with a nickel, and 50 cents to $10.00 when played with a quarter. It has our improved pay-out system. It cuts the coins out one at a time. It never pays out over or under the prize won.

A never-ending stream of nickels flowed through the slots of countless gambling machines all over America. Pre-eminent among manufacturers of such was the Mills Novelty Company, Chicago, which produced many different models. Above is shown the Mills Roulette, a variety made only in limited numbers (as evidenced by only a few surviving to the present time).

While some gambling machines used cents, dimes, or quarters (rarely higher denominations than that), most used nickels. Nickels truly were the "workhorse" coins of the American amusement and entertainment industry.

(From a 1902 Mills Novelty Company catalogue)

Bar Checks

We make a large variety of bar checks, either for use in machines which pay in trade or for any other purpose. We supply them in any size or quantity and with any style of lettering desired. We will take pleasure in quoting prices on application.

Gambling machines that paid out nickels were illegal in many areas in 1902, date of the above advertisement, so "GOOD FOR" trade tokens were dispensed instead. The theory was that merchandise, rather than money, was being given and, thus, gambling was not actually occurring! For numismatists this was to have a beneficial effect in later years, for the thousands of varieties of nickel-size brass tokens now in collectors' hands would never have been made were it not for numerous restrictive gambling laws.

The Caille Brothers Co.

1300-1350 Second Ave.

DETROIT, MICH.

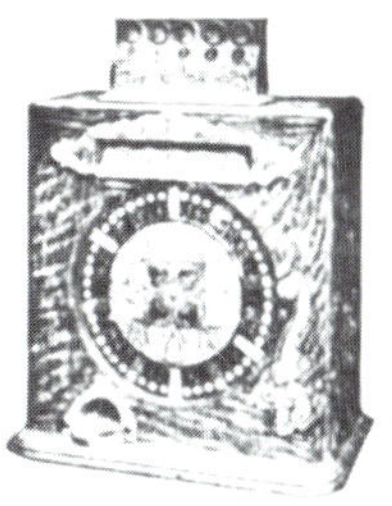

Ben Hur

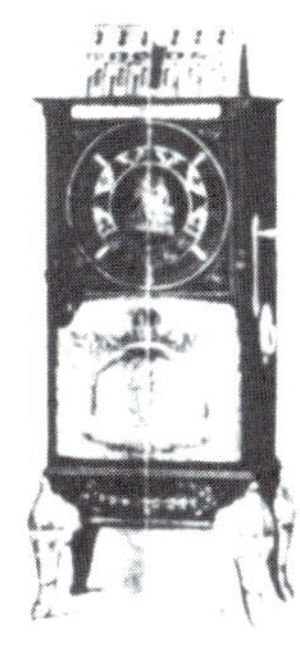

Puck

Lone Star

Centaur

Eclipse

Liberty Bell Gum Vender

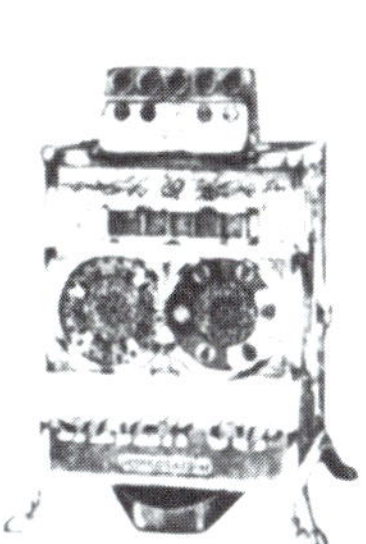

Silver Cup

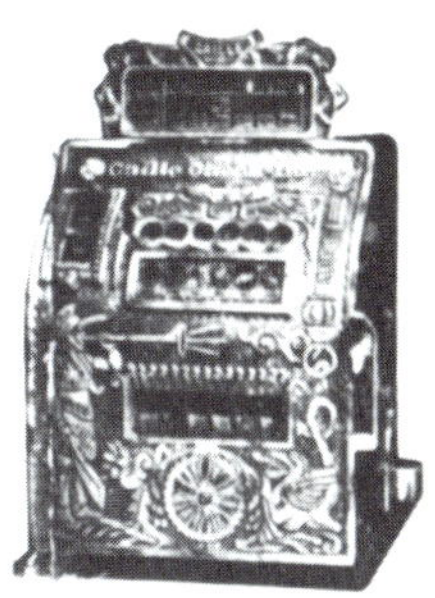

Check Boy

Baseball

The Caille Brothers Company was a distant second to the Mills Novelty Company in the field of slot machine manufacturing during the first decade of the present century. More so than the Mills products, the Caille gambling devices were remarkable for their ornate nickel-plated trim. Most of the machines shown here had a hearty appetite for Liberty nickels, but they could be order to accommodate other denominations if desired.

MAKE MINE MOXIE!

Or, What A Nickel Would Buy In 1885

July 15, 1984. Yes, 1984, 99 years after 1885. The alarm went off at 6:00 a.m., and 45 minutes later a mini-caravan consisting of an aging 1972 Cadillac Eldorado convertible, raspberry red, pulling a matching trailer, followed by another car headed toward Union, Maine, 156 miles distant. The trailer wasn't an ordinary trailer but, rather, was a calliope wagon. Inside was a National calliope, with 53 gleaming brass whistles, operated by perforated paper rolls, which could play "In the Good Old Summer Time", "Home on the Range", "They Cut Down the Old Pine Tree", "Put on Your Old Gray Bonnet", "Show Me the Way to Go Home", "There's a Hot Time in the Old Town Tonight", and other vintage tunes—loud enough that they could be heard a mile away (by actual measurement in an earlier trial run!). On the outside of the wagon letters in gold leaf proclaimed that the National-brand unit was made by the Harrington Manufacturing Company, Kansas City, Missouri, around 1921. The unit originally saw service with a traveling carnival in the state of Indiana, after which it passed to two Ohio collectors of automatic musical instruments, Roy Haning and Neal White, who restored it, after which it did a stint with Charles Kelton, White River Junction, Vermont, who used it in local parades. I acquired the calliope in 1983, had the wagon built for it, and first used it in the July 4th parade in Wolfeboro, New Hampshire that year.

On July 15th Union, Maine was the site of something very special: a gathering of Moxie memorabilia collectors and historians. What is Moxie? Old-time New Englanders know it well as a beverage that was once widespread in the northeastern section of the United States. Indeed, around 1920 Moxie outsold Coca-Cola in this district, so it has been said. Then Moxie faded from the scene—this was after World War II—and was almost forgotten. In recent years Moxie has become "rare" and can be found in only a few places.

During the late nineteenth century a nickel had many uses. There was the nickel beer, the five-cent cigar, and the nickel lunch. A nickel was apt to be a passport to a trolley car ride or the means of getting through the admission gates to an amusement park. Equipped with a handful of nickels, one could have a Saturday filled with fun.

Popular beverages, of which there were many, were apt to cost a nickel. Among these was Moxie.

Around 1884 Lieut. Moxie, about whom little biographical information has survived (even his very existence has been disputed by some), made a particularly fortuitous discovery while on "military maneuvers" near the equator, according to an early advertisement. The exact nature of this find was cloaked in secrecy, but it was said to have been a sugarcane-like plant with marvelous curative powers.

Lieut. Moxie's serendipity was translated into a commercial product bearing his name, Moxie Nerve Food. This potion, tasting bitter but with advantages of making it worthwhile, was advertised on an early bottle label:

"Contains not a drop of medicine, poison, stimulant or alcohol. But is a simple sugarcane-like plant grown near the equator and farther south, was lately accidentally discovered by Lieut. Moxie and has proved itself to be the only harmless nerve food known that can recover brain and nervous exhaustion; loss of manhood, imbicility and helplessness. It has recovered paralysis, softening of the brain, locomotor ataxia, and insanity when caused by nervous exhaustion. It gives a durable solid strength, makes you eat voraciously; takes away the tired, sleepy, listless feeling like magic, removes fatigue from mental and physical overwork at once, will not interfere with the action of vegetable medicines."

To a nation desiring recovery of manhood, reduction of imbicility, and other improvements, Moxie was a godsend. Sold as a fountain syrup and, particularly,

2 DOZEN
7-OZ
MOXIE
THE MOXIE COMPANY
BOSTON MASS
MOXIE

in green-tinted glass bottles, the nostrum achieved wide sales throughout New England and adjacent states. It was not without competitors. Ayer's Sarsaparilla, which numismatists will recall was advertised on encased postage stamps earlier (in 1862), had its own following as did Peruna syrup, Kilmer's Swamp Root (made in Binghamton, New York, by a medical doctor who was so successful that from the proceeds he built a large stone building across from the railroad station as well as a brick house, the latter serving today as a community center), Hostetter's Celebrated Stomach Bitters, and other products, not to overlook gadgets and treatments which were not masqueraded as soda pop or something to drink. Early advertisers of various remedies seemed to have difficulty with the English language, or at least they had their own interpretation of it. The difference between "invention" and "discovery" was not at all clear. Dr. Sanchez advertised widely that he discovered Oxydonor Victory, as one of many examples. And then there was a relatively new upstart product from Atlanta, Coca-Cola, which seemed to be claiming a good market share. Coca-Cola, it has been said, was first formulated in 1886, by which time Moxie was celebrating its first birthday (or perhaps its second, for other accounts place the origin of Moxie at 1884—noting, however, that it was not marketed until 1885).

Moxie was the brain child of Dr. Augustin Thompson, who hailed from Union, Maine. Moxie Nerve Food pointed the way to a good thing, and within the next decade or so such products as Moxie Catarrh Cure, Moxie Lozenges (which had advertising claims similar to those of Moxie Nerve Food), and even Moxie cigars made their appearance!

After the Civil War, Thompson moved his activities from Union, Maine to Lowell, Massachusetts, still later establishing facilities in Boston, New York, and Chicago. Moxie Nerve Food sales increased, but still Moxie was just one of many beverages. Then Thompson met up with Frank M. Archer and turned the publicity reins over to him. In Archer he found a genius. Moxie was catapulted from an ordinary beverage to the forefront as the thing to drink. Within a relatively short time the word Moxie was everywhere—painted on the side of buildings, in magazine and newspaper advertisements, on lapel pins, on collapsible fans, on children's toys, and even on shirts and umbrellas.

There was trouble in paradise, however, and the Pure Food and Drug Act, passed in 1906, forced Moxie and its competitors to refrain from health claims. Sufferers of softening of the brain and other maladies would have to turn elsewhere, and Moxie Nerve Food became simply Moxie, the soft drink.

In 1886 the Moxie Bottle Wagon made its appearance. Actually, there were several Moxie Bottle Wagons, but all had the same general appearance: a horse-drawn four-wheel cart with a large booth built in the form of an oversize Moxie bottle at the back. From within the booth a uniformed attendant dispensed drinks of the substance for a nickel each. Fourth of July parades, summer afternoons at the New England seashore, amusement parks, carnivals, old home weeks, and other events, celebrations, and locations saw the Moxie Bottle Wagon doing its thing. As part of the hoopla, aluminum tokens measuring an inch and a quarter in diameter were distributed in large quantities. On the obverse appeared a beautifully engraved depiction of the conveyance, with the inscription THIS IS THE MOXIE BOTTLE WAGON. The man within the bottle offers a glass to a young boy, while a girl looks on and three adults are in the background.

The reverse of the token consisted only of lettering: GOOD FOR ONE DRINK/MOXIE/AT THE MOXIE BOTTLE WAGON.

How many of these tokens were distributed? The number is not known, but it must have been thousands, for examples are seen with some frequency today. Nearly always they show signs of wear, with Very Fine and Extremely Fine being representative grades. In 1985, year of the Moxie centennial, on the numismatic market such a token was apt to bring in the $20 range, although a collector of Moxie, who was not a numismatist and who did not know about coin dealers, reported that he had been offered one for $600! Balancing this extreme example is a Moxie token acquired by the writer for just $1 in an antique shop in Bristol, Vermont in 1981.

The success of Moxie spawned many imitators. Of the situation the firm noted:

"During the last 40 odd years the Moxie Company and its predecessors have expended much effort and money in introducing Moxie to the public and establishing its legal rights in its trademark and trade name Moxie, with the result that millions of people know and like Moxie and it is in demand everywhere.

"This is what we have worked for and this confidence and public demand for Moxie has become an asset of tremendous value, the good will of our business.

"There is another result, however, of the great demand for Moxie, which seems as inseparable from popularity as shadow is inseparable from sunshine, namely: that unscrupulous manufacturers and dealers sometime substitute spurious imitation when Moxie is called for, imitate Moxie as closely as they are able in color and taste, and imitate the bottle of Moxie, considered it as a package, with its label, shape, color and distinctive appearance..."

A California firm came up with Toxie, an imitation, which was successfully challenged by Moxie, with the result that a judgment against Toxie was given in 1914.

In a contest aimed at striking down Proxie, another imitator, Frank Archer testified that more than a million and a half dollars had been spent in advertising Moxie and that "it is sold in almost every state of the Union," somewhat of an exaggeration, at least so far as the geographical territory is concerned. Court procedings revealed that "Moxie has a slightly bitter taste. It is also apparent that Proxie has a slightly bitter taste," and that the coining of the word Proxie, instead of the regular word proxy (the latter being part of the English language), testified to the intent to confuse the product with Moxie. Such copycats as Rixie, Modox, Non-Tox, and Noxie were struck down in the courts when Moxie's aggressive lawyers took action. One infringer, Ephraim Provo of Salem, Massachusetts, apparently suffered the indignity and embarrassment of being directed by the court to have his imitation bottles "publicly destroyed." (Wonder how many people watched the event?!)

The "slightly bitter taste" mentioned in the Moxie-Proxie court contest was either a Moxie advantage or a liability, depending on one's point of view. Not everyone liked the taste, and for this reason early advertisements sometimes bore the unusual phrase "Learn to drink Moxie," almost as if special training was required! Similarly, Moxie was billed as being "distinctively different." Moxie had its fans, and, apparently, complete loyalty to the beverage was required, or at least suggested, by extensive advertising which stated "Drink Moxie 100%."

By the 1940s Moxie was on the wane. Coca-Cola had long since achieved domination of the market. Pepsi-Cola, Nehi, Royal Crown and others became better known than Moxie. Frank Archer passed from the scene and, soon, Moxie was all but forgotten. Sure, an older generation of New Englanders would never forget it, but school children turned to other things. While many Liberty nickels and Buffalo nickels went to buy Moxie, fewer Jefferson pieces could make such a claim.

All was not lost, however. The Moxie trademark survived, and today one can buy cans and bottles of the stuff, although not for a nickel anymore!

Moxie memorabilia lives on. For numismatists there are aluminum Moxie tokens showing the Bottle Wagon, not to overlook countless old nickels which were probably once used to purchase the beverage, although well-worn nickels, like other circulated coins, keep their secrets well. For postcard collectors there are views of amusement parks, seaside resorts, and other locations with the Bottle Wagon or its successor (beginning in 1916) the motorized Moxie Horsemobile (which featured a model of a horse mounted on a car chassis). Old Moxie bottles abound, particularly in New England antique shops. Hand-held cardboard fans featuring Muriel Ostriche, Lillian MacKenzie, and other pretty girls are as nice to look at

Proxie and Modox were two of the many imitations that Moxie struck down in the courts.

today as they were back in 1916 (the copyright date). Pins, buttons, tip trays, metal signs, and other remembrances are likewise avidly collected.

The spirit of Moxie lives on, and when I and my caravan pulled into the fairgrounds in Union, Maine on July 15th, the celebration was well under way. My friends Eddie and Brenda Clark, who had introduced me to Moxie lore and collectibles in the 1970s, were already on hand and had mounted a gorgeous exhibit of old-time memorabilia. Bob and Muriel Heath, residents of Union who were among the sponsors of the celebration, had a nice exhibit, as did Ken Shure, John Baker, and several others, including the Matthews Museum, located in Union, which had just begun collecting Moxie things.

The calliope and its towing car were pulled into place in a grassy spot, and after a few minutes of assembly, "Put on Your Old Gray Bonnet" started the music program which could be heard all over the fairgrounds. A popcorn stand, refreshment area, and flea market contributed to the general conviviality. Then at 2:00 p.m. a parade—with Eddie Clark and me in the car and calliope leading it—formed. Both of us had a feeling of posterity which is hard to translate in print—here we were leading a procession in the first-ever Moxie collectors' celebration. Augustin Thompson would have been proud to have seen the several dozen antique cars and other conveyances trouping down the parade route in his memory. As it was, an old oil painting bearing his image, the property of the Matthews Museum, was hung nearby among the Moxie memorabilia exhibits.

An hour later, having bought some Moxie centennial T-shirts and other remembrances of the event, my caravan headed back to New Hampshire. I paused to reflect that the Moxie celebration is typical of the traditional America one reads about in history books or vicariously enjoys in Norman Rockwell illustrations but which can be seldom experienced in person. It was not a lavish event, the dusty fairground and homespun surroundings were the very antithesis of "high society," and there was no business to be transacted, unless hot dogs and popcorn are counted—but everyone had a really wonderful time.

A Typical Instance of a Customer's Vigilance and the Result

MISS SHAW'S LETTER

Cathance Lake, Cooper, Maine.
August 13, 1917.

The Moxie Company,

Dear Sirs:

On August seventh I bought three bottles of Moxie at Harry Lombard's store, in Meddybemps, Maine. When I got them back to the camp I noticed they were *without* labels and each bottle had the same sort of cap to it. (I am sending you one of the caps.) One of the bottles was without doubt a regulation Moxie bottle, stamped with your mark, but the other two were marked "Four Crown Soda Water, Clark's Harbor, N. S., M. A. Nickerson." They all contained the same kind of drink (imitation Moxie) which made two members of the party extremely ill for about six hours.

We have been drinking Moxie all our lives and it has never before made us ill.

I do not wish to make any claims but I do hope that you will follow this up, for the vile stuff was bottled in one of your bottles which I will be glad to send to you upon request. My reason for writing this is to save someone else a similar experience.

Very sincerely yours,

S. F. SHAW.

OUR ATTORNEY'S REPLY

Boston, September 20, 1917.

Miss Sarah F. Shaw,
Machias, Maine.

Dear Madam:—

Your letter addressed to The Moxie Company, dated August 13th, was referred to us by the company for investigation of the matter therein mentioned. We immediately sent an inspector to interview Mr. Lombard, and learned from him that he was selling a beverage put up by Walter J. Commins, of Calais, Maine, which had the appearance of genuine Moxie. Of course, as is usual in such cases, he denied having sold any of the Commins beverage upon a call for Moxie. After the preliminary investigation, Mr. Brennan, of this office, went to Calais on August 25th, and there conferred with Mr. Commins and his attorney, Richard J. McGarrigle, Esquire. The result of this visit is that we have put a quick and effective stop to this case of infringement on the Moxie Company's rights. We have the signed admission of Mr. Commins that he made and sold the infringing beverage, and we also have his agreement to immediately stop the putting up and sale of such beverage, coupled with a provision for the destruction of the imitation Moxie bottles. This conclusion of the matter is as effective as an injunction of the court, and we have no doubt but what, under the advice and guidance of his counsel, that Mr. Commins will keep his promise. We also communicated with Mr. Lombard, and have a similar statement from him. We have told him that a letter of apology is due to you and if you have been put to any expense for medical service or otherwise, on account of the sale of this spurious beverage to you, that he should properly compensate you. For this purpose, we have given him your name and address, and we shall be interested to know whether he does in fact adopt our suggestion.

On behalf of our clients, The Moxie Company, we wish to thank you for calling this matter to our attention. Our client takes a just pride in its good reputation, which has been built up at the expenditure of enormous sums of money and the uniform high quality of its product. Your action in this matter has been of great benefit, not only to the Moxie Company, but to the general public, because by putting a stop to Mr. Commins' fraudulent dealing, you have doubtless saved many other persons the unpleasant experience which you had, following the drinking of the inferior imitation of Moxie.

Yours very truly,

OLIVER MITCHELL,

MITCHELL, CHADWICK & KENT,
Attorney for the Moxie Co.

Attorneys for the Moxie Company were always ready to pounce on any suggestion of imitation or wrongdoing, as this 1917 exchange dramatizes.

The nickel remained king of the amusement business throughout the 1930s. In 1932, the depth of the Depression, slot machines, jukeboxes, pinball machines, and other nickel-operated devices did extremely well.

The above 1932 advertisement from "The Billboard" offers "unequalled luxury" for just $3. My, what inflation has done in the years since then!

Illustrations on the next several pages are also from "The Billboard," December 1932.

One! Two!! Three!!! Four!!!!

"AUTOMATIC 5 JACKS"

MAKES 5 TIMES ITS COST IN A WEEK WITHOUT HALF TRYING

EVERYBODY'S TALKING LIKE THIS:

"Your new All-Aluminum 'Five Automatic Jacks' is the classiest looking, snappiest acting, surest shooting money-maker I've ever handled. Averaged $32.00 last week," says SAM A...., of ILL.

"NUF SED!"

Here's the Description

- 5 Big Jackpots Crammed With Gold and NO 'JAM' on Payout.
- 3000 5c Sales—and NO 'CLOG' on Punchout.
- Each Jackpot 'Dumps' Automatically and Readily.
- Each Jackpot Automatically Controlled to Protect Profits. (5 Controls on $10 Jackpot—2 Controls on Each of the 4 $5 Jackpots.)
- Profit Is IN When Jackpots Pay OUT.

●● ***All This in a Brilliant, Glittering All-Aluminum Case—Securely Sealed and Absolutely Tamper-Proof.***

Here's the Set-up:

TAKES IN—3000 5c Sales.		$150.00
PAYS OUT: 1 Big $10 Jackpot (set on 5 controls)	$10.00	
4 $5.00 Jackpots (each set on 2 controls)............	20.00	
25 Seals	15.00	45.00
30 WINNERS.........PROFIT......		$105.00

OPERATORS: DON'T 'MISS THIS TRAIN.' . . . COSTS ONLY $6.50 each. In All Quantities. Terms: Cash with order, or C. O. D. F. O. B. Chicago.

GARDEN CITY NOVELTY MFG. COMPANY
4327 E. Ravenswood Ave., Chicago, Ill.

A nifty profit was turned by those setting up nickel punchboards. According to the mathematics shown above, an investment of $45 yielded a $105 profit, not bad any time, but certainly fantastic in 1932 when this enticement was printed.

The Watling Manufacturing Company, Chicago, was primarily a manufacturer of slot machines for gambling, but they also made coin-operated scales and, as shown above, pinball machines. (1932 advertisement from "The Billboard")

New York Coin Machine Operators!

COME . . . SEE THE LATEST MACHINES AT OUR EXHIBIT

Booths No. 5, 6, 7, NAAP Convention
Pennsylvania Hotel
32d St. & 7th Ave., New York City
November 28-December 3

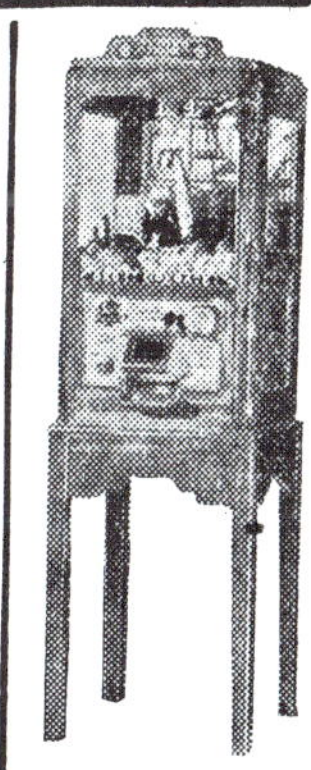

JUNIOR CRANE
Hand-Operated.

Make Real Money With "Mutoscope" Traveling Cranes

Steady incomes being made weekly by operators all over the country. Get in on these permanent money-makers now. Write us for circulars and full particulars.

37 Years of Successful Manufacturing of Coin Operated Machines.

It It's Automatic We Have It

INTERNATIONAL MUTOSCOPE REEL CO., Inc.
451 West 31st St., New York
Telephone: LOngacre 5-4793.

This coupon entitles you to our special Christmas Billboard offer. Good only until December 15th.

Name ....

Address ....

....

The International Mutoscope Reel Company derived its name from the Mutoscope, a coin-operated peepshow marketed around the turn of the century. By 1932, when the above advertisement appeared, these devices were obsolete, and the company made other gadgets for entertainment and amusement, including the Traveling Crane, most familiarly known as the "Iron Claw." The patron putting a nickel in the slot could grasp at all sorts of prizes—perhaps a watch, perhaps a silver dollar, perhaps a piece of jewelry. As you might expect, many players came close, but few succeeded in winning anything valuable.

Visits to the Mint

During the 19th Century

Visitors to the Philadelphia Mint in 1853 saw silver three-cent pieces and half dimes being made, together with many other denominations. On the following pages you are invited to take a tour of the Philadelphia Mint in 1853, and then again a number of years later—through the medium of sketches created at the time.

An 1853 Visit to the Mint

In 1853 "Gleason's Pictorial Drawing Room Companion" sent a reporter and artist to the Philadelphia Mint. An article, now slightly excerpted and corrected for errors, was printed:

"We give some very fine scenes descriptive of the United States Mint at Philadelphia. They are given with great accuracy and beauty by our artist, Mr. Devereaux. The United States Mint was founded in 1792, and the business of coining commenced in 1793, in the building occupied at present by the Apprentices' Library. It was removed in 1830 to the fine building it now occupies in Chestnut Street above Olive Street. The edifice is of white marble, and the north front opposite to Penn Square is 123 feet long, with a portico 60 feet long, of six Ionic columns, and the south front on Chestnut Street has a similar portico.

"Since the enormous influx of gold from California, the United States Mint has become an object of more than common attention and interest, and the place is usually filled with visitors, watching the various processes with which the metal goes through before it comes out a finished coin. The machinery and apparatus by which these are accomplished are of the most complete and perfect character. The rooms in which the smelting, refining and alloying are done are spacious apartments in which a large number of workmen are employed. Heaps of rich ores are to be seen laying around, as they were extracted from the mines, or gathered in dust from the sands and mountain streams of California. Bars of the pure metal, representing many thousand dollars in value, are passing through hands which, like those of Midas, seem to turn what they touch into gold. The heat of this place is insufferable; fires glow with the intensity of those in a foundry; the men are as smutched and dust-begrimmed as those in a smithery; There is a suffocating sensation of hot air, steam and perspiration penetrating the atmosphere, which is anything but pleasant to experience, when the thermometer is palpitating under a summer temperature.

"Crucibles are handled with iron tongs and cotton mittens, the metal is shaped into bars and then reduced to the requisite fineness. All of this takes place in one apartment. In another there is a most beautiful steam-engine which drives the rolling and stamping machinery. This engine is of one hundred horse power and works the rolls, draw benches and cutting presses. It is called a steeple-engine and has two cylinders. It is worked by boilers 40 feet in length and 40 inches in diameter, which also works a ten horse and five horse engine in the separating and cleaning apartments. This main engine is of the most elegant workmanship, polished like a piece of cutlery, and works without the least perceptible jar.

"From this room the visitor walks into that where the rolling machines are at work, turning out the metal to the proper degree of thickness which each particular denomination of coin requires. The metal is cast into ingots 14 inches in length, and about 5-8ths in thickness; they are then rolled to very near the proper thickness, when they are passed through the draw-benches to equalize them; the strips are then cut at the presses; these presses cut out from 200 to 260 a minute. There are 14 men employed in this room—two for each pair of rolls.

"The pieces cut are then passed to the Adjusting Room. Here each piece is weighed separately and adjusted with a file. Light and imperfect pieces are remelted. There are 54 females employed in this room. The pieces are then taken to the Milling and Coining Room. There are from 200 to 400 milled in a minute, according to their size.

"In another department the coins are cut with a punch the desired size and then stamped. The coins are placed by a person seated at the machine, in a perpendicular tube, down which they descend, one at a time, being seized as they drop,

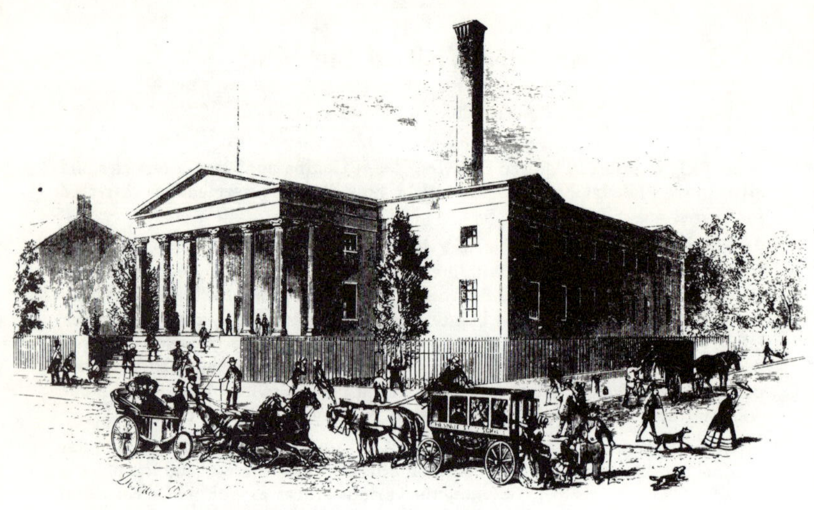

EXTERIOR VIEW OF THE UNITED STATES MINT, PHILADELPHIA.

Exterior of the Philadelphia Mint. This and the next three illustrations are from "Gleason's Pictorial Drawing Room Companion," 1853, where they illustrated a feature article.

GENERAL PRESSING AND CUTTING ROOM OF THE UNITED STATES MINT, PHILADELPHIA. (See p. 40 for description.)

In this room ingots were rolled into strips and planchets were produced. Operations of the Philadelphia Mint remained essentially the same from 1836, when steam power was introduced, until the mint transferred to a new facility shortly after 1900.

ADJUSTING ROOM OF THE UNITED STATES MINT, PHILADELPHIA.

Fifty-four women were employed to weigh silver and copper planchets and to file any excess metal from them so as to render them suitable for coinage.

PRESSING AND MILLING ROOM OF THE U. S. MINT, PHILADELPHIA.

Several coining presses are shown in the background. The device on a pedestal to the lower left is a milling machine for putting raised rims on blank planchets prior to striking.

by part of the machinery, which pushes the coin under the stamp, once it falls under the machine into a glass-covered box. This part of the process used in former years to be performed by a press, which still remains in the building, works by a lever and screw, requiring eight men to laboriously work at it; now the process requires scarcely any manual labor but handling the pieces of coin. The repetity with which the pieces are executed is surprising—being at the rate from 75 to 200 per minute. Cents, dollars, eagles, double eagles are turned out with equal facility, the process being the same in all.

"Some idea of the extensiveness of these operations may be had when it is stated that in one month, lately, nearly three million pieces of gold, silver, and copper were coined, and that nearly $4 million in value is coined every month. In addition to the other attractions of the Mint there is a most extensive cabinet of coins, ancient and modern, which is one of the greatest curiosities probably to be met with no where else in the country. The officers of the Mint are polite and attentive to visitors, and endeavor to make their visit one of instruction as well as amusement. It is under the very effective management of Mr. Dale, the director.

"We have more than ordinary satisfaction in presenting so very fine a series of engravings as those we give of the U.S. Mint. They are critically correct, are our readers may rely upon their truthfulness as our artist, Mr. Deveraux, passed no inconsiderable period of time in making the necessary drawings for the series, within the walls of the Mint, assisted by the gentlemanly and urbane director and officers of the institution. Any of our readers who may now happen to visit Philadelphia will go to the Mint understandingly, and there can test the truthfulness of our illustrations, and at the same time doubly enjoy the subjects of investigation in this interesting institution, from having been hereby familiarized with the operations, machinery, and the appearance of the eternal economy of the Mint—one of the largest in the world."

VISITING THE PHILADELPHIA MINT

"Harper's Weekly" sent an artist, V. Gribayedoff, to the Philadelphia Mint to sketch various coining processes. Shown on this and the next several pages are mint operations as they appeared to visitors during the late nineteenth century.

ABOVE: An early step in the preparation of coins was the casting of ingots from molten metal. This was primarily done with silver and gold; nickel and copper were often contracted for outside of the Mint.

At the Rolling Bench

By means of passing through successive rollers, the ingots were formed into lengthy strips.

The strips were then taken to the drawing bench where they were drawn to uniform thickness.

ABOVE: Two different types of planchet-cutting machines were in use. Disks were punched from metal strips like a cookie cutter would punch dough.

BELOW: The punched disks were passed through the milling machine where they received an upset or raised rim. This resulted in less metal movement during the later coin striking process and permitted sharper pieces to be struck.

ABOVE: A lady operator tended a belt-driven coining press while onlookers observed the process.

LEFT: Prior to shipment, coins were counted and placed in cloth bags.

"Destroying Coin Dies at the United States Mint in Philadelphia" is the caption on this illustration which appeared in the December 28, 1889 issue of "Frank Leslie's Illustrated Newspaper." This was the last year of the nickel three-cent piece, and presumably, all dies for that denomination were destroyed, as were other dies dated 1889.

Index

Index